THE LONELY GOD

Ronald L. Dart

Wasteland Press
Shelbyville, KY USA
www.wastelandpress.net

The Lonely God
by Ronald L. Dart

First Printing – December 2005
ISBN: 1-933265-80-9

Unless otherwise indicated, Bible quotations in this book are
taken from the Authorized King James Version of the Bible.

Printed in the U.S.A.

Table of Contents

1

The Paradox

*Thus saith the LORD, Let not the wise man glory in his wisdom,
neither let the mighty man glory in his might, let not the rich man
glory in his riches: But let him that glorieth glory in this,
that he understandeth and knoweth me, that I am the LORD
which exercise lovingkindness, judgment, and righteousness, in the
earth: for in these things I delight, saith the LORD
(Jeremiah 9:23-24).*

For as long as I can remember, I have believed in and thought
about God. Like a lot of people, I have had my ups and downs, my
moments of clarity and my bouts with doubt. But over time I came to
realize that if I was to have any hope of understanding God, I would
have to get used to truth being expressed in paradoxical terms. We've
all heard the old canard, "The Bible contradicts itself." It doesn't
really, but there are times when the truth runs sharply counter to what
we think, and it is often presented to us in the form of a paradox – a
statement that is seemingly contradictory or opposed to common
sense, and yet is true.

We have trouble with this, in part, because of the way modern
man thinks. The people who first received the books of the Bible
were much more comfortable with paradox. The western mind has to
explain everything, even things it does not really understand. The
oriental mind realizes that there are some truths that defy rational
explanation and are better taken as they stand.

The difficulty also arises out of the fact that a complete understanding of God in real terms extends beyond the grasp of the human mind. That is not to say that God is a mystery, but that the mind has limitations that aren't easily transcended. One scientist observed that the universe is not only stranger than we imagine, it is stranger than we *can* imagine. So it is with God. This leads me to conclude that Jeremiah is saying that we can understand God, not at the cosmic level, but at a practical level that the human mind can grasp. Jeremiah suggests that there are specific things about God that we can understand and that these are the important things.

Against Jeremiah's statement is this one from Solomon. "He has made everything beautiful in its time. He has also set eternity in the hearts of men; yet they cannot fathom what God has done from beginning to end" (Ecclesiastes 3:11 NIV).

The different versions of the Bible seem to struggle over this verse, but it serves the purpose in saying that there are limits to our understanding. The Hebrew word *owlam*, here rendered "eternity," comes from an old root that means, "to veil from sight." It is the vanishing point, the place where two parallel lines seem to meet in the distance, the point where something disappears from sight. We can look back in time and accept that God has always existed. But we cannot imagine how that can be. We can't resist thinking about it, because God has placed it in our minds. But he has done so in a way that leaves us unable to grasp the idea from beginning to end – doubtless because there is no beginning and there is no end.

There was a time when I thought that if I just studied the Bible long enough and carefully enough, I could answer all the big questions and put them together in a way anyone could understand. It was a foolish idea and I am glad to be rid of it. It has freed me up to talk about God in whatever terms he sees fit to reveal himself. And if some of that revelation seems paradoxical, so be it.

This does not mean that we cannot know or understand God. Far from it. What it means is that we can know and understand him *only on his terms*, not ours. And if God seems paradoxical, we would serve ourselves well to keep an open mind and take him that way. The paradox may only exist in our own mind.

This book is not an attempt at a unified theory of God nor an attempt to argue for this or that dogma. It is a conversation about

God. It is possible that I will answer some questions about God that have troubled you. It is certain that I will raise some new questions to take their place. My objective is to share the journey toward understanding, to walk alongside you and talk about God. And perhaps, dare we think it, to find friendship with God.

A note on Bible references: Unless otherwise noted, scriptural citations are either from the King James Version or the New King James Version. The difference between the two is obvious. Other translation abbreviations are, NIV - New International Version, NRSV - New Revised Standard Version, NASB - New American Standard Version.

2

The Lonely God

And God stepped out on space
And he looked around and said
"I'm lonely, I'll make me a world."[i]

It is a simple, almost elegant cosmology. The poet, James Weldon Johnson, not only sees God as Creator of everything, he imagines a *motive* for the act of creation. It is a thought that emerges as something of a surprise, but God didn't create all this on a whim. He had something in mind and if we are to know him at all, we have to start with God as Creator.

It may seem strange to think of God as lonely. But if we believe that God created all things and was uncreated himself, then we must believe that there was a time when God was alone and was not content to stay that way. The Bible tells us that God is eternal. He has always existed and always will. So the 14 billion year age of this universe is nothing at all in God's time. This universe is merely a project. And before this universe, Johnson imagined that God was alone.

Yes, I know there were angels. But angels are *created* beings. Before the angels, God was alone. It seems unthinkable. God, through eons of time, sitting alone, the only light in the darkness. This is surely not true, but we will never be able to penetrate the darkness between us and the time before time. Whatever went on in that time, God was pursuing more than a hobby when he started the project that included us. At some level, Johnson was right. He continued:

And far as the eye of God could see
Darkness covered everything,
Blacker than a hundred midnights
Down in a cypress swamp.
Then God smiled,
And the light broke,
And the darkness rolled up on one side,
And the light stood shining on the other,
And God said: That's good!

Science now tells us that the physical universe is 13.7 billion years old, plus or minus a bit. Thanks to a space probe, they also can tell us that the universe will always expand and never collapse. So according to the latest science, 14 billion years ago there was nothing but darkness. The poet said God smiled. The Bible says that he spoke. The result was the same. One minute there was nothing; the next minute there was light. Some call the first split second of that minute "The Big Bang." Light travels at 186,000 miles per second, so at the end of the first minute, light had penetrated over 11 million miles into the darkness.

Both poet and Bible draw an absolute distinction between light and darkness and this is important. God called the darkness night and the light day. The poet says that darkness and light stand opposite. They are not the same thing. The darkness is not light and the light is not darkness. This is called "antithesis." It is important to know this from the outset, because in some forms of convoluted reasoning, men have a way of confusing light and darkness. God is not amused:

"Woe unto them that call evil good, and good evil;
that put darkness for light, and light for darkness;
that put bitter for sweet, and sweet for bitter! Woe
unto them that are wise in their own eyes, and
prudent in their own sight!" (Isaiah 5:20-21).

Thanks to that space probe, they now say that the universe is "flat," that is, it is expanding at a steady rate and will continue to expand forever. There will be no "big crunch," with the universe collapsing in on itself. The implications are awesome. The universe is not permanent. Nor is it part of an eternal cycle of collapse and expansion. Fourteen billion years ago there was nothing. And at some time billions of years into the future, the universe will use up all its fuel and burn out. It is a temporary phenomenon. It arose in darkness and it is rushing outward into darkness.

Further, there is no way to explain the origin of light. No way, that is, except the way of the Bible and the poet. God said "Let there be light," and there was light, driving darkness away to stand on the other side.

I suppose Stephen Hawking is right when he says it is useless to try to imagine the time before time. He called the big bang a "singularity" where both time and space began, and said that it was impossible to look beyond the singularity. Since both space and time began at the singularity (assuming I understand what Hawking is saying), then there is no "before" that we can see.

That said, there had to be a "before" and while nothing of the time *before* time is revealed or discoverable, we can draw some inferences about that time from what happened on this side of the singularity and from what is revealed to us by God.

For example, we know from the Bible that God made a decision to create man. "Let us make man in our image," said God. It never occurred to me that God was alone when he said this, and the Hebrew tends to confirm it by using a plural form for God: *Elohim*. Yes, I know that most consider *Elohim* a "divine we" and that it actually means God in the singular. But as a kid I still wondered who God was talking to when he made this declaration. Yes, he could have been talking to himself as I might, standing by my wheelbarrow, shovel in hand muttering, "Let's plant these roses, now." Nevertheless, we have to remain open to the possibility that God was talking to another participant in the creation process.

Whatever the case, there was a prime decision: "Let's make man." That decision required other decisions concerning the nature of man and the nature of an environment fit for man. The process of making those decisions created a plan. And while we imagine that

God exists outside of time, any statement that God does one thing before another suggests that, while God may exist outside of *our* time, he creates his own time.

Surely the first decision of the Lonely God was the nature of man, because everything else flowed from that. The creation of light made it possible for man to see. The creation of air made it possible for him to breathe. The creation of food made it possible for man to eat. Angelic beings would have required none of that.

In the process of creating man, God said something quite revealing. Having said that everything he had made was very good, he said concerning man, "It is *not* good for the man to be alone." And in saying this, God may have revealed something about himself. Man was created in the image of God. And if it was not good for man to be alone, then perhaps it was not good for God to be alone either.

> *So God created man in his own image, in the image of God created he him; male and female created he them. And God blessed them, and God said unto them, Be fruitful, and multiply, and replenish the earth, and subdue it: and have dominion over the fish of the sea, and over the fowl of the air, and over every living thing that moveth upon the earth (Genesis 1:27-28).*

Man was created male and female and in the image of God. Maybe this suggests a feminine side to God. Or maybe it says something else about God. Since man was made to reproduce himself, God was also able to reproduce himself and was doing so in man. The means whereby God reproduces himself is the act of creation followed by human reproduction. There will be many hitches along the way, but the motive of God is revealed right there on the pages of Genesis. He was starting a family, the essential cure to loneliness.

The very idea of God being lonely is unthinkable because it seems impossible that an infinite God should find himself wanting anything. But unless we can think along these lines, we are left with a God who created from no need, no want, no desire. Even saying that God had a purpose in his creation is to say that his purpose would have been left unfulfilled without the creation. God would have lacked something that he desired.

It was *space* that moved Johnson to postulate a lonely God, and it was space that moved the Psalmist to think about God's motive in creating man:

> *When I consider your heavens, the work of your fingers, the moon and the stars, which you have set in place, what is man that you are mindful of him, the son of man that you care for him? (Psalms 8:3-4).*

Then the author of Hebrews comes up against the same question. He has been examining the relationship of the Son of God to the heavenly beings whom he calls "angels." Man could have been made an angel, but he was not. Why then, Paul wondered, were the angels created?

> *But to which of the angels said he at any time, Sit on my right hand, until I make thine enemies thy footstool? Are they not all ministering spirits, sent forth to minister for them who shall be heirs of salvation? (Hebrews 1:13-14).*

Like the servants on a great plantation, the angels are not the heirs. They are *servants* to the heirs. And in what is almost an aside, Paul [ii] reveals that God has heirs. Failing to grasp this simple truth, or denying it, closes much of the Bible to our understanding, because we miss the *purpose* in it all. We human beings, struggling along like grubworms here below, are destined to become *family* with God.

> *Beloved, now are we the sons of God, and it doth not yet appear what we shall be: but we know that, when he shall appear, we shall be like him; for we shall see him as he is (1 John 3:2).*

Now I hasten to add that I do not believe God was alone from eternity. But, as most of us have learned, one can still be lonely in a crowd. If God was not alone, then there are some other questions we have to explore.

---

i. From "The Creation," by James Weldon Johnson.

ii. After considering carefully the discussion of the authorship of the letter to the Hebrews, I have concluded it was most likely Paul who wrote it.

3

Open to God

Truths turn into dogmas the moment they are disputed – Chesterton

There is no explanation of God offered by man that can do anything but diminish God. And the further we go in trying to explain God, the further we go down a cul-de-sac. The creation of dogma is a major barrier. If we don't stay *open* to him, to his revelation of himself, we can never hope to understand. Dogma closes that door.

God is. God is what he is regardless of what we think or say. And God presents us with questions we cannot hope to resolve with dogma. We have to take him as he reveals himself to us over time, or we can never know him at all.

But who am I talking about when I speak of God this way? For the most part, when we speak of God, people will think of the one Jesus called, "Father." But it soon becomes apparent that the word "God," in the Bible, means more than that. Consider how God is introduced to us:

> *In the beginning Elohim created the heaven and the earth. And the earth was without form, and void; and darkness was upon the face of the deep. And the Spirit of Elohim moved upon the face of the waters. And Elohim said, Let there be light: and there was light (Genesis 1:1-3).*

I am using the Hebrew word for God, *Elohim,* for a reason. The word is plural. It is the plural of Eloah which means a god or the God. We keep stumbling over words when we talk about God because in our language, *as in Hebrew,* the word "god" has more than one meaning. In one passage, *elohim* even refers to devils: "They sacrificed unto devils, not to Eloah; to *elohim* whom they knew not, to new *elohim* that came newly up, whom your fathers feared not" (Deuteronomy 32:17).

Now there is nothing especially hard about this. We commonly use the word "god" to refer to the real God and to other gods. We know the difference by the context. The Hebrews did the same thing. What is difficult is the use of the *plural* for the one God. I have already noted the argument that the plural in this case is an idiomatic way of referring to the One God. But that leaves some questions unanswered. A lot of the confusion arises because of the choices made by biblical translators, and because of English usage of the word "god." For example, in the laws regulating slavery, there is this example:

> *And if the servant shall plainly say, I love my master,*
> *my wife, and my children; I will not go out free: Then*
> *his master shall bring him unto the judges [Hebrew:*
> *elohim] (Exodus 21:5-6).*

The New International Version and the *King James Version* both render *elohim* as "judges" in this passage, while the *New American Standard Bible* and the *New Revised Standard Version* say that he will bring the man before God. So we have a semantics problem with the word God both in Hebrew and in English. We might do well to put this question on the shelf for the time being and read a little further in Genesis:

> *And Elohim said, Let us make man in our image, after*
> *our likeness: and let them have dominion over the fish*
> *of the sea, and over the fowl of the air, and over the*
> *cattle, and over all the earth, and over every creeping*
> *thing that creepeth upon the earth. So Elohim created*
> *man in his own image, in the image of Elohim created*

he him; male and female created he them (Genesis 1:26-27).

Now if you are the inquisitive sort, you may wonder who God is talking to when he says, "Let *us* make." And this is an example of the kind of problem we create for ourselves when we try to explain too much about God.

There are two poles in the discussions of the nature of God. One, which encompasses most of mainstream belief is the doctrine of the Trinity – the belief that God is three persons in one Godhead. The other pole argues that the Trinitarian view is polytheistic and insists that there is only one God and that he is one, not three. Both points of view present us with difficulties.

Think about this in terms of the creation. The Apostle John said, "All things were made by him; and *without him was not any thing made that was made*" (John 1:3). So taking John in the plainest terms possible, anything that exists either has always existed or was made by God. Everything that is was made by him. And if there is no one else who is eternal, then before creation, God existed alone.

The way some people see it, 7000 years ago, God lived alone in solitary splendor (or, if you are scientifically inclined, 14 billion years ago). Then he created everything out of nothing. But before that, for all of eternity, God was alone. From what we know of God from the rest of the Bible, that makes no sense at all, but never mind. It doesn't have to make sense to us for now.

But just suppose for a moment that God was *not* alone. Take the context of John's statement on creation. It is in the opening remarks of his Gospel:

> *In the beginning was the Word, and the Word was with God, and the Word was God. The same was in the beginning with God. All things were made by him; and without him was not any thing made that was made. In him was life; and the life was the light of men. And the light shineth in darkness; and the darkness comprehended it not (John 1:1-5).*

At first blush, this seems to be a conundrum. How can he be

with God and be God at the same time? It is not a problem if we accept as fact that the Hebrew word *Elohim* is plural. The Word was God and was with God. There were two who were called God. So it makes perfect sense for God to say, "Let *us* make man in *our* image." God was not alone.

Now the mind that can't deal with paradox comes to a dead end here. If there are two who are called "God," then God is not one but two. And if there are two Gods, then we are suggesting polytheism. Early Christian thinkers could not accept that, and were driven to think of God as a Trinity, only one God who is three persons in one "Godhead." Never mind that this is nowhere stated in the Bible. To the western mind, it had to be that way to be rational. In the Old Testament, God was severely presented as One. Then, the Gospel presents Jesus as the Son of God which suggested that he was also God. The Jews therefore considered Jesus' claim to be the Son of God as blasphemy.

This came to a head one day as the Jews kept pressing Jesus on his identity. "How long dost thou make us to doubt?" they insisted. "If thou be the Christ, tell us plainly".

> *Jesus answered them, I told you, and ye believed not: the works that I do in my Father's name, they bear witness of me. But ye believe not, because ye are not of my sheep, as I said unto you. My sheep hear my voice, and I know them, and they follow me: And I give unto them eternal life; and they shall never perish, neither shall any man pluck them out of my hand. My Father, which gave them me, is greater than all; and no man is able to pluck them out of my Father's hand. I and my Father are one (John 10:24-30).*

Now how should we take this last statement? Jesus was on earth and his Father was in heaven, so they are plainly not the same person. This puzzle is answered in the doctrine of the Trinity by concluding that the "Godhead" is composed of three persons who are one God. If that is a little hard to grasp, you can take comfort in knowing that people who believe it call it a mystery. "Godhead" is a word coined to take in the idea of a Triune God.

It may be a little easier if we can think of God in his own terms. And the way Jesus describes the relationship is in terms of family – Father and Son. God is one *family* with more than one member of the family.

But there is no question how the Jews took Jesus' statement. They started picking up stones to throw at him. When he asked them which of his good works deserved stoning, they replied: "For a good work we stone thee not; but for blasphemy; and because that thou, being a man, makest thyself God" (John 10:33).

To the Jews, there was but one God. And for Jesus to claim to be the Son of God was, to them, tantamount to claiming divinity for himself. Jesus then goes straight to the semantic difficulty presented by the word "god." The Jews should have known this.

> *Jesus answered them, Is it not written in your law, I said, Ye are gods? [i] If he called them gods, unto whom the word of God came, and the scripture cannot be broken; Say ye of him, whom the Father hath sanctified, and sent into the world, Thou blasphemest; because I said, I am the Son of God?"*

So, how many Gods are there? According to Paul, only one.

> *As concerning therefore the eating of those things that are offered in sacrifice unto idols, we know that an idol is nothing in the world, and that there is none other God but one. For though there be that are called gods, whether in heaven or in earth, (as there be gods many, and lords many,) But to us there is but one God, the Father, of whom are all things, and we in him; and one Lord Jesus Christ, by whom are all things, and we by him" (1 Corinthians 8:4-6).*

This troublesome little passage actually points us in the right direction. How is it possible for there to be only one God and yet many gods *in heaven*? What Paul is saying in his own way is that the problem is mere semantics. There is one God, who is the Father. At the same time, there are many who are called *elohim*. The word

"God" is used in two distinct ways and only discerned by the context. And because Paul recognizes the semantic difficulty, he qualifies his "one God" statement by explaining that there is but "one God the Father." This is the one most of us refer to when we speak of God. And in that sense, there is indeed only one God.

So far, so good, but what about these *elohim* in heaven? Who are they? I don't know, but there is a suggestion in a fascinating description of God's throne in Revelation. There was one sitting on the throne whose appearance, as best John could describe it, was like an opaque crystal that radiated a green iris of light around his throne. Arrayed around this throne were 24 other thrones upon which were seated 24 "elders," all clothed in white and wearing crowns (Rev. 4:4).

Who are these people and what are they doing there? In the Bible, elders are judges and judges are *elohim*. These all have crowns and their seats are called thrones. The place

The Orthodox Church explains it this way:

"First of all, it is the Church's teaching and its deepest experience that there is only one God because there is only one Father.

"In the Bible the term "God" with very few exceptions is used primarily as a name for the Father. Thus, the Son is the "Son of God," and the Spirit is the "Spirit of God." The Son is born from the Father, and the Spirit proceeds from the Father -- both in the same timeless and eternal action of the Father's own being.

"In this view, the Son and the Spirit are both one with God and in no way separated from Him. Thus, the Divine Unity consists of the Father, with His Son and His Spirit distinct from Himself and yet perfectly united together in Him."

– www.oca.org

fairly crackles with power, and there are creatures around the throne who sing praises to God. When they do, the 24 elders rise from their seats, fall before the throne of God and cast their crowns down before him.

This place is alive with power. And it is populated with, what, spirit beings? Would we dare call them *elohim*? We might, but let's not decide that yet. Let's put it on the shelf while we continue to think it through.

The author of the Book of Hebrews takes some pains to develop our idea of God. God, the author says, spoke in time past to the fathers through the prophets. Now, in these last days, he has spoken to us by his Son. The Son of God has been appointed heir of all things, and it was by the Son that the worlds were made (Hebrews 1:2).

It is apparent as you read the first chapter that the Son of God is a different class of being from the angels. God never said to any angel, "You are my Son, this day have I begotten you." The relationship is totally different. The angels are to worship the Son. What follows is a stunning revelation.

> *But unto the Son he saith, Thy throne, O God, is for ever and ever: a sceptre of righteousness is the sceptre of thy kingdom. Thou hast loved righteousness, and hated iniquity; therefore God, even thy God, hath anointed thee with the oil of gladness above thy fellows (Hebrews 1:8-9).*

The speaker says to the Son, "Thy throne, O God . . ." The Son is addressed as God. Then, in a surprising turn, the Son is told that God, *even his God*, has anointed him. The Son is God and has a God. Even the structure of this sentence is revealing. The "*even thy God*" is necessary because he has addressed the *Son* as God. I know it is awkward, but by my math, that makes two Gods.

Are we polytheists, then? No, because although there are many who are called *elohim*, we acknowledge only one because only one is supreme. At this point the discussion can dissolve into endless arguments over the semantics of God, but let's not go there.

We know that the Father is God. We know that the Son is God. We know that they are one. We know that the Holy Spirit is one with them. Does that make us Trinitarians? By one definition, it might. By another it might not. Does it mean that we are polytheistic if we believe in more than one who is God? By one definition, it might. By another it might not.

I can't think of a better example to show the uselessness of hanging labels on people. On the other hand, I have to admit, tongue in cheek, that it may be useful in excommunicating people who disagree with us.

But the author of Hebrews is not finished. He has more to say about this. If the angels are a different sort of being from the heir, what is their role? He answers, "Are they not all ministering spirits, sent forth to minister for them who shall be heirs of salvation?"

Angels, heavenly messengers, are the servants on this great plantation. We are the immature heirs of the plantation. Jesus obtained his more excellent name by inheritance. We will finally do the same. John addressed this in a letter.

> *Behold, what manner of love the Father hath bestowed upon us, that we should be called the sons of God: therefore the world knoweth us not, because it knew him not. Beloved, now are we the sons of God, and it doth not yet appear what we shall be: but we know that, when he shall appear, we shall be like him; for we shall see him as he is (1 John 3:1-3).*

It is this passage that led C.S. Lewis, among others, to conclude that it is the destiny of man to become God. And by that, I think he meant, we shall become *Elohim*.[ii]

The rigid "one God" dogma precludes all that. It even denies the divinity of Jesus himself and denies that he ever existed before his human birth. But Jesus himself dashed that idea. He told the Jews that he had known Abraham. "Your father Abraham rejoiced to see my day," Jesus said, "and he saw it, and was glad" (John 8:55-56).

The Jews were mortified. "Thou art not yet fifty years old," they exclaimed, "and hast thou seen Abraham?" Jesus replied: "Before Abraham was, I am."

There was no mistaking what Jesus intended by this. The Jews understood all too well. They started gathering stones to kill Jesus for blasphemously claiming to be God.

Yes, Jesus was the Messiah, but he was much more than that. Yes, he was a great teacher, but he was much more than that. But he could be neither the Messiah nor a great teacher *if his central claim is untrue*. Jesus claimed to be the Son of God in that special way that made him God in the flesh.

I began with the first chapter of John, and I return there.

Having established that the Word was not only with God but was God, John went on to say, "And the Word was made flesh, and dwelt among us, (and we beheld his glory, the glory as of the only begotten of the Father,) full of grace and truth."

Must we become the captives of our own dogma? Or Can we remain open to God?

---

i. From Psalm 82:6.

ii. C.S. Lewis, "Mere Christianity, Counting the Cost."

4

How Many Gods?

*I tell you the truth, the Son can do nothing by himself;
he can do only what he sees his Father doing,
because whatever the Father does the Son also does
(John 5:19 NIV).*

No one in any mainstream faith is prepared to believe there are three Gods. That would make them polytheists like the Greeks and the Romans. But early Christian theologians had a problem to face that Jewish theologians never had to deal with. As I. A. Dorner put it, "It is a plain matter of fact that none who have depended on the revelation embodied in the Old Testament alone have ever attained to the doctrine of the Trinity."[i]

But in the New Testament, the earliest theologians of the church had to deal with a simple fact. Jesus is God and he acknowledges the Father as his God. By any normal reckoning, that leaves us with two Gods. Add the Holy Spirit, and you have three Gods or, a Trinity.

But then there arises another problem. The Bible does not present us with two religions, old and new. In reading the New Testament, we never encounter any sense that the writers saw any difference between their conception of God and that of the Old Testament writers. Nor is there any hint that they thought they were the pioneers of a new religion – that is, the preachers of a new God.

So how were the early theologians to maintain a strong, monotheistic faith in the face of more than one God? After no small debate, they concluded that God is a Trinity, one "Godhead" in which there are three "coequal" persons. But that didn't solve all their problems. *The International Standard Bible Encyclopedia* (ISBE) summarizes the dogma and the problem it poses.

> The term "Trinity" is not a Biblical term, and we are not using Biblical language when we define what is expressed by it as the doctrine that there is one only and true God, but in the unity of the Godhead there are three coeternal and coequal Persons, the same in substance but distinct in subsistence. And the definition of a Biblical doctrine in such un-Biblical language can be justified only on the principle that it is better to preserve the truth of Scripture than the words of Scripture.[ii]

So the Trinity is a dogma that is not formulated from the *words* of scripture, and that is a highly problematic idea for most Christians. We like to think that the truth of Scripture is in the words. It follows that the doctrine of the Trinity is a post apostolic development because the Apostles never spoke of it. How, then, did the post apostolic church fathers come to the doctrine? There was what the ISBE calls a "determining impulse," and a "guiding principle."

> The *determining impulse* to the formulation of the doctrine of the Trinity in the church was the church's profound conviction of the absolute Deity of Christ, on which as on a pivot the whole Christian conception of God from the first origins of Christianity turned. *The guiding principle* in the formulation of the doctrine was supplied by the Baptismal Formula announced by Jesus.
>
> It was by these two fundamental principia – the true Deity of Christ and the Baptismal Formula – that all

attempts to formulate the Christian doctrine of God were tested, and by their molding power that the church at length found itself in possession of a form of statement which did full justice to the data of the redemptive revelation as reflected in the New Testament and the demands of the Christian heart under the experience of salvation.

This appears to be the entire underpinning of Trinitarian dogma as formalized in later years by the church fathers. First, the absolute deity of Christ, second, the "baptismal formula" given by Jesus. [iii] So, where is the proof of the Trinity?

The fundamental proof that God is a Trinity is supplied thus by the fundamental revelation of the Trinity in fact: that is to say, in the incarnation of God the Son and the outpouring of God the Holy Spirit. . . [iv]

What they are saying is that they came to the doctrine of the Trinity by what they see as fairly obvious facts. One, the coming of God in the flesh as Jesus, while still acknowledging the Father in heaven as God. That makes two who are called God. Finally, by the outpouring of the Holy Spirit, which by their reckoning made three.

But we still have not seen how they avoided the epithet "polytheism." That was a very real problem in the early church where heresies were springing up like so many weeds. The oneness of God is asserted so firmly in Scripture that it led some to conclude that it was simply not possible for Jesus to be God, thus resolving the problem in the opposite direction. The assault on the deity of Jesus that followed may have forced the issue and led to a decision that would carry its own problems into the future.

The question on the table, then, is whether in describing God as a Trinity the early fathers arrived at the best solution to the problem they faced. Here, as is so often the case in theological studies, we are victimized by semantics, the meaning of words. Paul warned against being overly reliant on words, [v] and most religious arguments are bedeviled by bickering about words. But if we take, not only the facts of the Bible, but the words as well, the Bible may solve the problem for us in words altogether familiar.

The words are "Father" and "Son." These words are known in all generations, in all languages and in all cultures. Not only are the words familiar, but the *relationship* is understood. Notice above that the doctrine states that Father and Son are the same in substance. That is, they are both Spirit. Further, the doctrine states that they are "distinct in subsistence," in other words, they are two distinct persons.

This is familiar to us in human terms. My dad and I were both flesh, but we existed as two distinct persons. So what about the "Three in One" idea? Once again, if we decide to use the words of the Bible to describe the facts we see there, we run squarely into the family again: "For this cause shall a man leave his father and mother, and shall be joined unto his wife, and they two shall be one flesh." [vi] So two can be one after all.

No one has a problem with the unity of the family, even though we have two persons composed of the same substance, flesh. In biblical terms, two can be one, so why create a new set of words to explain an old fact. Now I fully understand that there are long and complex arguments on all sides of this question. But most people realize intuitively that the simplest explanation is more likely to be right. Here, the simplest explanation is that God is a family composed, for now, of a Father, a Son, and a Family Spirit.

Thus we find our oneness, and we explain the relationships. In any family, the Father and Son are equal in many ways, but not all. The Father is always the Father and the Son is always the Son. These are not identical roles, and in an effort to explain this relationship, we turn to the words of scripture.

"The Father loves the Son," said Jesus, "and has given all things into his hand" (John 3:35). The Father gives. The Son receives. The Father has turned everything over to the Son. The early Christian theologians had to fight off heresies on all sides, and here they encountered "subordinationism." Technically, subordinationism is, "A doctrine that assigns an inferiority of being, status, or role to the Son or Holy Spirit within the Trinity."

But it isn't necessary to see inferiority in the relationship between Father and Son. In a family, the father is first among equals. The answer may be that simple. Jesus described the relationship in terms of family. This is a long citation, but it deserves careful study.

I tell you the truth, the Son can do nothing by himself;
he can do only what he sees his Father doing,
because whatever the Father does the Son also does.
For the Father loves the Son and shows him all he
does. Yes, to your amazement he will show him even
greater things than these. For just as the Father
raises the dead and gives them life, even so the Son
gives life to whom he is pleased to give it. Moreover,
the Father judges no one, but has entrusted all
judgment to the Son, that all may honor the Son just
as they honor the Father. He who does not honor the
Son does not honor the Father, who sent him.

I tell you the truth, whoever hears my word and
believes him who sent me has eternal life and will not
be condemned; he has crossed over from death to life.
I tell you the truth, a time is coming and has now
come when the dead will hear the voice of the Son of
God and those who hear will live. For as the Father
has life in himself, so he has granted the Son to have
life in himself. And he has given him authority to
judge because he is the Son of Man (John 5:19-27
NIV).

We have to decide how we are going to take this important passage. First, Father and Son do not operate independently, but together. Father and Son have no secrets from one another. They love one another. Both deserve the same honor from men. Both can raise the dead. There is one thing the Son does that the Father does not now do: judge men. There is a reason for this. It is because Jesus is the Son of Man. That idea does not see full development until later.

None of this is very difficult if we don't have to fight off heresies. Passages like this invite the specter of subordinationism, but nothing here suggests that the Father is anything other than first among equals. In any family, someone has to lead. In the divine scheme of things, it is the Father. This does not make the Son an inferior being. Imagine a father with four sons, working together in the field. Father and sons are all equal in terms of their faculties and their ability to work. But the Father is first among them.

So, if we can forget about the various heresies, we can say that God is a *family*, composed of Father and Son, accompanied by the Family Spirit. [vii] This allows us to understand God on his terms instead of ours.

But that leaves us with the "Family Spirit" to think about, and here we step into an area not so familiar. The Holy Spirit does not appear in terms of family. The Spirit is not a son, daughter or consort. While the Father and Son are revealed in human terms, the Spirit is not. The only visual manifestations of the Spirit in the New Testament are "a bodily shape like a dove," (Luke 3:22), and as "tongues of fire" (Acts 2:3).

The King James translators of the Bible took a singular step to call this to our attention – I suspect it was intentional. The idea of the Holy Spirit is not new in the Bible. The Old Testament speaks often of the movement and activity of the Spirit of God. But the scholars who opened up the Greek to make the text of the New Testament available to us seem to have realized they had something new on their hands. The actions and involvement of the Spirit reached an entirely new, and more personal level in the New Testament. For whatever reason, they overwhelmingly adopted the term "Holy Ghost" in preference to "Holy Spirit."

Whatever a ghost is, at least in the English language, it is disembodied. In the case of the Father and Son, we have persons who are revealed in bodily terms. The Spirit of God is not. It is a divine wind, the breath of God. It may be useful to point out that in both Greek and Hebrew, the words for "spirit," *pneuma* and *ruach*, may also be used for the wind that blows the leaves on a tree.

What shows up in the New Testament is something entirely new to man. Not that the Spirit of God was unknown, but it was never known this way nor, as far as we know, was it ever a *Parakletos*, a counselor, an advocate, an intercessor, an advisor.

So the scholars had to find a way to express this distinction, and they chose the old English "Ghost," I suspect because they saw the Spirit as real, but disembodied. I should add one caveat. Don't worry about the pronouns used for the Spirit ("it" instead of "he"). In the Greek, the pronouns must agree with the gender of the noun. *Pneuma*, the word for "Spirit" in the Greek, is a neuter noun.

Now let me proceed to define the problem. At one point in his ministry, Jesus made a cryptic statement about the Holy Spirit, calling it "living water." We know he meant the Holy Spirit because John adds this note: "By this he meant the Spirit, whom those who believed in him were later to receive. *Up to that time the Spirit had not been given*, since Jesus had not yet been glorified" (John 7:39 NIV).

This statement is more important than it seems, because it is plain that the Holy Spirit had been active up to this point in the same way it was in the Old Testament. In old times, The Holy Spirit "came upon" people, or they were "filled with" the Spirit of God. And when Mary and Joseph brought the baby Jesus to the Temple for the first time, an old man was there who had been brought there by the Spirit of God. His name was Simeon, "and the Holy Ghost was upon him." He came to the Temple on this special occasion, "by the Spirit," and prophesied concerning this child, "the Lord's Christ" (Luke 2:25 ff.).

So what could John have been driving at when he said that the Holy Spirit had not been given? Plainly the Holy Spirit was present and working all through the Old Testament and into the New. Nothing had changed.

Anyone with a good concordance can make his way through a study of the Spirit of God in the Old Testament, but don't look for the expression, "Holy Ghost." It isn't there. Rather, the same Spirit is called "the Holy Spirit" (only three times), "the Spirit of God" (14 times), and "the Spirit of the Lord" (26 times). And there are other synonyms, and parallel expressions that refer to the Spirit in other ways.

It is interesting to compile a list of the characteristics, the properties, of the Holy Spirit in the Old Testament. A partial list includes:

- It could reside in a person, as an abiding presence, as specifically with Joseph (Genesis 41:38).
- The abiding presence could be taken away, as David feared (Psalm 51:11).
- It "comes upon," falls on, or fills a person, all in a transitory sense, i.e. it comes and goes in terms of its influence – as with Balaam (Numbers 24:1-2).

- It can overwhelm normal behavior, as with Saul, but only in a transitory way (1 Samuel 19:18-24).
- It could inspire craftsmen and artisans for the work of the Tabernacle (Exodus 31:1-5).
- It could speak with the tongue of a man, as with David (2 Samuel 23:1-2).
- It can tend to run in families, according to Isaiah, but obviously conditionally (Isaiah 63:7-11).
- It can be vexed (Isaiah 63:7-11).

You can probably add to this list with a little study of your own, but this will serve for now. But we must ask the next question: What do we see in the New Testament that we did not see in the Old? What are the characteristics, the properties, of the Holy Spirit in the New Testament?

- It is an active agent for God (Luke 1:34-35).
- The Holy Spirit in particular can be blasphemed (Matthew 12:31-32).
- The Holy Spirit speaks (through men), but it speaks, (Mark 13:11).
- The Holy Spirit filled people on special occasion, this was transitory (Luke 1:41).
- The Holy Spirit was "upon" people (Luke 2:25-26).
- It revealed things to them (Luke 2:25-26).
- It could actually appear in bodily form, though not human like form (Luke 3:22).
- You could be baptized with the Holy Spirit (Acts 1:5).
- The Holy Ghost is exactly the same thing in the New Testament as it was in the Old (Acts 1:16).
- The Holy Spirit is a source of power (Acts 1:8).
- The Holy Spirit is a gift of God (Acts 2:38).
- The Holy Spirit calls, commissions and sends people to a work (Acts 13:1-4).
- The Holy Spirit directs that work in some detail (Acts 16:6-7).
- The spirit hears from God and speaks what it hears to us (John 16:13).

There is much more, but this will serve to illustrate that the Holy Spirit is a constant in both Testaments. The early Christians seem much more aware of the Spirit, but after Pentecost, who can be surprised at that?

But why, then, would John say that the Holy Spirit was not yet given? And why would Jesus later speak of the coming of the Spirit as a future event, "But when he, the Spirit of truth, comes, he will guide you into all truth. He will not speak on his own; he will speak only what he hears, and he will tell you what is yet to come" (John 16:13 NIV).

An answer to this, along with some new questions, is suggested in that wonderful conversation Jesus had with his disciples after the Last Supper.

> *If you love me, you will obey what I command. And I will ask the Father, and he will give you another Counselor to be with you forever – the Spirit of truth. The world cannot accept him, because it neither sees him nor knows him. But you know him, for he lives with you and will be in you" (John 14:15-17 NIV).*

At first blush, this last seems like a distinction without a difference. But there is something entirely new here. The Holy Spirit has not heretofore been described as a *Counselor*. Perhaps what John is saying is that the Holy Spirit had not yet been given as *Counselor*.

As Jesus continues this conversation, it becomes apparent that the Counselor is not just another way of speaking of the Father or the Son. He makes it plain that the Counselor is the Holy Spirit, and that it is *sent by* the Father.

> *All this I have spoken while still with you. But the Counselor, the Holy Spirit, whom the Father will send in my name, will teach you all things and will remind you of everything I have said to you (John 14:25-26 NIV).*

Later, Jesus will say, "When the Counselor comes, whom *I will send to you from the Father*, the Spirit of truth who goes out from the Father, he will testify about me" (John 15:26). The coming of the Holy Spirit as Counselor is a future event at this point, and the Counselor is *sent from* the Father and Son. It is something distinct from the two of them, but completely at their command.

In fulfilling the role of Counselor, the Holy Spirit is absolutely dependent upon Christ. Still later, Jesus will say: "Because I have said these things, you are filled with grief. But I tell you the truth: It is for your good that I am going away. *Unless I go away, the Counselor will not come to you*; but if I go, I will send him to you" (John 16:6-7 NIV).

The "Counselor" in the Greek is *parakletos*. No other New Testament writer uses this form of the word. And John only uses it in one other place, to refer to Jesus: "And if any man sin, we have a *parakletos* with the Father, Jesus Christ the righteous" (1 John 2:1).

So, are the Holy Spirit and Jesus the same thing? Hardly. The Holy Spirit is Jesus' *agent* in the world. Whatever the Holy Spirit does, Jesus is considered to have done. It is much the same as the Holy Spirit being the agent of the Father in the begetting of Jesus. Mary was with child of the Holy Spirit, and yet the Holy Spirit was not deemed to be the Father.

So the Holy Spirit was present when Jesus spoke of its coming in the future. But the Spirit was to be sent by Jesus in a new role, that of counselor, advocate, guide. In a sense, he was to be the family attorney. What changed from the Old Testament was the *relationship* of the Spirit to the servants of God.

So the Spirit was with them and would be in them. What did that mean in practical fact? It meant that the Holy Spirit was their guide, the one who shed light on the choices they had to make. He stood with them and closed one door while opening another. The Spirit is still here, still in us, and still doing the same thing, unless dismissed or ignored.

Luke and Paul were so aware of the work of the Spirit in their life and work, that when the Spirit closed a door, they knew it was the Spirit that did it. They didn't have to guess. How could they tell? Because they were looking for it. They were listening for it, trusting for it.

So what does all this tell us about the Trinity? Are there three Gods or one "Godhead" with three persons in it? The question is almost entirely lost in semantics, but we can draw some conclusions based on the *words* of the Bible. What men call "the Trinity," is a *family*, composed for now of Father, Son and the Family Counsel. All may be called God. All are eternal. The Father is first among equals.

Surely, God is much more than this, but the rest is not revealed. And on the matter that is not revealed, your guess is as good as mine.

---

i. *International Standard Bible Encyclopedia*, article, "Trinity."

ii. Ibid.

iii. "Therefore go and make disciples of all nations, baptizing them in the name of the Father and of the Son and of the Holy Spirit" (Matthew 28:19 NIV).

iv. *ISBE*, article, "Trinity."

v. "Of these things put them in remembrance, charging them before the Lord that they strive not about words to no profit, but to the subverting of the hearers" (2 Timothy 2:14 KJV).

vi. Ephesians 5:31 KJV.

vii. Or, if you are so inclined, you may say the Trinity is a family, composed of Father, Son, and Holy Ghost.

5

The Design

Then God sat down
On the side of a hill where He could think;
By a deep, wide river He sat down;
With His head in His hands,
God thought and thought,
Till He thought,
"I'll make me a man!"[i]

It wasn't like this, of course, but this is poetry. And it is certain that at some point in what one might call "time," God did make this decision. And nothing is clearer than the fact that God started with a comprehensive design. I became profoundly aware of this remarkable truth in the most ordinary way.

I have to see my eye doctor three times a year, and I am always left waiting in his examination room. The walls there are covered with pictures and diagrams of the human eye. I often gaze at these pictures with something approaching religious awe. The eyes that I see all around the walls were *designed*. And surely no one could fail to see that.

It was one particular diagram that started me thinking. It was a simple vertical cross section of the eye with everything named. It was there to help the doctor explain things to his patients. The chart itself was designed to make things as simple as possible, so it was easy to pick out the different parts of the eye.

I already knew what rods and cones were. A navy school explained that to me so I would understand night vision. Rods and cones are the light sensors arranged around the back of the eye in the retina. There are millions of them in each eye. Light enters the eye through the cornea, passes through the lens, and is focused on the surface of the retina. When light strikes the rods and cones, a tiny electric current is generated. The current travels along fibers to the optic nerve, hence to the vision center in the brain, and we see.

It sounds simple enough. At least that's what I thought until I noticed that there were 150 million rods and cones, and only one million fibers in the optic nerve. When we look at an object, an image is projected on the retina and stimulates all 150 million rods and cones. Each of them has to carry its own message to the brain so we can see the entire image that is projected there. Simple math tells me that 150 different signals have to travel down one optic nerve fiber. How is the traffic handled?

Having a basic knowledge of electronics, I knew that you could carry multiple messages down one wire, but those messages all have to be coded in such a way as to be properly directed and understood at the other end. I wondered how the coding was done.

I decided to ask my doctor when he finally came in. He thought for a minute and said, half joking, "Well, there is this tiny computer chip behind the eye." We had a little laugh over it, and he went on with the examination. But I was not satisfied. I knew there was no computer chip, and I wanted to know how it was done. When I got home, I took my *Britannica* to my favorite chair, propped up my feet and started reading.

Much to my surprise, it turned out that my doctor was not joking after all. There really is a computer chip of sorts. It is not in the brain, where you might expect it to be. It is in the retina itself. The sensors of the eye, the rods and cones, are not hard wired into the brain. Behind the sensors is a network of interconnected nerve cells. I learned that groups of rods and cones are connected together in networks, and that the signals received by one influence the signals sent by another. Some signals are strong, and others are suppressed. The result is that the image we finally see is, in reality, "*computer enhanced.*"

If you look at a fine black line on a white piece of paper, the image of the line that strikes the retina is relatively broad and composed of shades of gray. This is because the optics of the eye are not geometrically "perfect." In the nature of things, diffraction of light spoils the perfect image. The spread of light from the white areas into the black has to be corrected, so the tiny computer chip in the retina *enhances the contrast*. The rods that receive more light inhibit the nearby rods that receive less, and the resulting transmission to the brain is a fine black line.

If you have ever played with lenses, you may have noticed a phenomenon called "chromatic aberration." It is a property of the lens that it focuses different colors of light at different lengths. The result is a margin of colors around the image created by the lens. As you look at a white object against a black background, the lens in your eye created just such a halo of color around the image on your retina. But you do not see it, because the little computer chip in the back of your eye suppresses it. The Designer wanted you to have a nice clean image to consider.

But that is not all the little computer does. Take the problem of panning, for instance. We know that if we take a movie or video camera and sweep it from one object to another (called a "pan"), that the result is a dizzying blur. Why doesn't that happen when we sweep our eyes from one object to another? Try a little experiment. Stand in front of a mirror and look at your own eyes. Look first at one and then shift your gaze to the other. If you are like most people, you will not see your eyes move. What happens is that the little computer chip in the back of your eye momentarily suppresses vision. You only "see" when the eye stops.

It is a nice little design touch. We aren't troubled with blurs as we move our gaze from one object to another. Try it. Scan the room where you are sitting. What seems like a camera pan is, to the eye, a series of steps, each accomplished neatly and without thought. Actually, it is more than a nice touch. It is an integrated part of a designed system of vision.

Another surprise came when I learned that individual sensors do not always send a steady message to the brain. In fact, if the retina is steadily and evenly illuminated, there is very little going on in the optic nerve. Some of the sensors in the retina act like "on" switches, and others like "off" switches. The result is that the brain is not bombarded with unnecessary information. When light strikes a set of rods, a message tells the brain that the light is on. The rods don't bother telling the brain anything until something changes. But the brain keeps telling you the light is on, even though nothing is coming up the optic nerve. This is how 150 million sensors can make do with 1 million "wires" to carry the message. They don't use the wires all the time. Also, each rod and each cone has its own identity code, and ends up directed to its correct place in the vision center of the brain even if it is part of a mass of messages from many rods and cones.

While we rarely think about it, the eye is in constant movement. Some of that movement is so small it is hard to detect. But the eye must move to see. You may think you are staring fixedly at some object, but your eye is making tiny movements all the time. If you were able to fix your unmoving gaze on a black spot, it would disappear in a few seconds. The rods and cones adapt to the stimulus and switch it off. So it is necessary to move the eye enough to cause the image to fall on a new set of rods and cones every few seconds. And yet this must still keep the object in the center of your gaze without giving the impression of movement. All this is microscopic and "computer controlled." You could not stop the movement if you tried.

Did you know you have a pulley in your eye? Of course you know that you have muscles that move your eyes. You are conscious of them when you move your eyes to extreme limits both vertically and horizontally. There are four of these on each eye, positioned above, below, and on each side of the eye. One would think that was enough, but there are two other muscles that run through "pulleys" and enable the eye to *roll* in the socket. If you tilt your head toward your shoulder, these muscles act to keep the eye vertical. One more nice little touch of design.

But the Designer of the eye had other problems to solve. Of special importance is the fact that the amount of light striking a rod or cone is quite small, too small to provide the energy to create an electrical charge. How then, does the retina sense light? Through a simple chemical process. When exposed to light, the chemical substance of the retina breaks down into two other substances and generates the energy to turn the switch on. It takes about a half-hour in the dark for the chemicals to recombine – the period of dark adaptation.

We see through a complicated set of optics, a chemical reaction, computer enhancement, brain interpretation, and more. The eye turned out to be much more complicated than I had imagined. But the eye is useless alone. It is a part of *system of vision.*

Television is also a system for managing images. A video camera is useless by itself. It needs a system of cables, modulation, amplification, broadcast, reception, and display to be of any use at all. The same is true of the eye. The images that fall on the retina must be processed and transmitted to the vision center of the brain to mean anything.

In a video camera, an image is projected by a lens onto sensors in the back of the camera. This image is picked off in a series of sweeps by a beam of electrons and is coded and sent along a cable to a video screen. Here, a beam of electrons sweeps across a screen (in older systems, 400 to 600 lines per screen, depending on the system) and causes microscopic spots to glow in color. This produces an image on the television screen for us to "see."

It is significant that the video system "sees" nothing. It simply transmits an image to be seen. The image is not real, it is just glowing dots on glass. Your dog does not see what you see when it sits in your lap and watches television with you. Animals sense movement and sound, but unlike you, they see no depth in the screen. In fact, you don't either. But your system is designed and trained to *interpret* what you see on a flat screen in terms of depth and texture. The dog's is not.

In the eye, an image is focused on the retina where it is sensed by 150 million rods and cones, computer enhanced and adjusted, sent to the brain and merged with the image from the other eye. But this combined image is not projected onto a screen to be seen. These images are processed by the brain and create in your mind, not a picture of the world around you, but the world itself. Look around. What you see is not a picture, it is real. You can move into it. It has texture, depth, color. Objects are related to one another in space. You can walk over to a table and touch it. It is precisely where you saw it to be. You will be able to predict how it will feel by the way it looks.

There are those who would tell you that all this evolved without conscious direction from a designer. They point to a wide variety of eyes, from the simple to the complex, and argue that development up the scale is possible. And yet, there is no evidence that such an evolutionary process ever took place nor any reason why it should have.

Furthermore, the eye is part of a *system of vision*. The eyes of birds, bats, fish, dogs and cats are all part of intricate combinations of complex subsystems. No part of these systems is of any value without the other parts. And no part of one system is of any value with another system. A bird would not profit from the eye of a fish. Having the eye of a man would not profit a dog. The hound would still lack the mental capacity to make use of what he could see. The human system of vision might actually make it hard for a wolf to survive. He needs his particular combination of senses to hunt, to eat, to live. Phillip Johnson in his book, *Darwin on Trial*, summarizes nicely:

> Some single celled animals have a light-sensitive spot with a little pigment screen behind it, and in some many-celled animals a similar arrangement is set in a cup, which gives improved direction-finding capability. The ancient nautilus has a pinhole eye with no lens, the squid's eye adds the lens, and so on. None of these different types of eyes are thought to have evolved from any of the others, however, because they involve different types of structures rather than a series of similar structures growing in complexity. [ii]

Evolutionists admit being baffled by the nautilus, "which in its hundreds of millions of years of existence has never evolved a lens for its eye despite having a retina that is practically crying out for this particular simple change." [iii]

The eye did not evolve blindly. It was designed. It was designed by someone who himself could see, "He that formed the eye, shall he not see?" (Psalm 94:9).

When I took my encyclopedia back to the shelf, I placed it there with a sense of awe. Because that short article made it completely impossible for me to believe that such a system for seeing could evolve on its own. It was designed by an intelligence who knew that there was something to see. And he gave it to man, because he wanted man to see it.

For You formed my inward parts;
You covered me in my mother's womb.
I will praise You, for I am fearfully and wonderfully made;
Marvelous are Your works, And that my soul knows very well.
My frame was not hidden from You, When I was made in secret,
And skillfully wrought in the lowest parts of the earth.
Your eyes saw my substance, being yet unformed.
And in Your book they all were written, The days fashioned for me,
When as yet there were none of them.
How precious also are Your thoughts to me,
O God! How great is the sum of them! (Psalms 139:13-17 NKJV).

---

i. "The Creation," James Weldon Johnson.

ii. *Darwin on Trial*, Philip Johnson.

iii. Ibid.

6

The Choice

And the LORD God planted a garden eastward in Eden;
and there he put the man whom he had formed.
And out of the ground made the LORD God to grow
every tree that is pleasant to the sight, and good for food;
the tree of life also in the midst of the garden,
and the tree of knowledge of good and evil (Genesis 2:8-9).

The story of the Bible begins and ends with a tree. In the Garden of Eden, the Tree of Life held the central place. After the expulsion of man from the garden, we don't hear of the tree again until the last book of the Bible. There, man is in a very different environment called, "The paradise of God." Once again the Tree of Life is central. But now there is not one tree of life, but twelve. They are on both sides of the river of life and they bear twelve kinds of fruit. Moreover, the leaves of the tree are for the healing of all people.[i] It is those who do God's commandments who have a right to the Tree of Life, and the permission to enter the City of God.

Everyone knows that the Tree of Life was in the Garden of Eden. It is also important to know that the Garden of Eden was not everywhere. It was a little world of its own within the larger world of the planet. It did not even encompass all of Eden, but was "eastward in Eden." The brief geography of Eden is unfamiliar, but this was a very long time ago and much has changed since then. It was surely a beautiful garden. Every tree that was good for food and pleasant to the eye was there; God made them grow out of the ground.

Then God created man out of the dust of the ground put him in this small world. For reasons that will become apparent, it is important to know that God placed Adam and Eve in a little world of their own. They were not exposed to the dangers of the whole world, but protected in a garden of God's making and design.

There are a few things we can say about this world. We know there were animals there, but none of them were dangerous. We know that there was all the food anyone could ever desire. There was work to do, because Adam was told to "dress and keep" the garden. We know the climate was mild because there was no need for clothes. The man and his wife were naked, and there was no shame in it. [ii]

There was no downside in Adam's world. From what comes later, we know there were no thorns or briars, and we can infer that there were no weeds or noxious plants. We can also infer that there was no pain, no disease, and we know there was the potential of living forever. It was an altogether perfect little world.

But there was a way out of this world into a larger, very different world, and that way was in the form of a tree. Why would anyone want to leave a perfect world, a paradise like Eden? It's a good question, and the answer may be as simple as this: Adam and Eve were not prisoners. They were not specimens for God to keep in his own private zoo. They were *entirely human* and entitled therefore to freedom and dignity. So there had to be a way out. There had to be a *choice* of worlds to live in. But at the first, Adam and Eve were completely unaware of this other world. Their eyes were not opened to it.

Now about this other tree. It was called "the tree of the knowledge of good and evil," and it was placed squarely in the center of the garden right alongside the tree of life.[iii] And the Lord told the man, *"You are free to eat from any tree in the garden; but you must not eat from the tree of the knowledge of good and evil, for when you eat of it you will surely die" (Genesis 3:3).* Now we know that God did not mean Adam would drop dead if he ate of the tree, but that he would become subject to death from that day forward. Adam was human and physical and, without access to the tree of life, his life was limited. He would grow old and die.

God told Adam and Eve plainly not to eat of the one tree. But if he didn't want them to eat of it, *why was it there*? Sure, it was a beautiful tree, but let's not imagine that God could not make the tree beautiful and safe at the same time. The answer seems obvious enough. The tree was there because man had to have a choice. If paradise became stultifying to him, he could leave. The tree was his way out, and it was not placed in some obscure corner of the garden. It was right there in the center alongside the Tree of Life. It gave man *a choice of worlds to live in.*

We don't know how long Adam and Eve were in the garden before the temptation by the serpent. It was probably long enough for them to get bored. But when the encounter takes place, we start filling in some blanks about this tree.

The serpent seems almost surprised to see the tree there and in such a prominent place, so he asks the woman, "Yea, hath God said, Ye shall not eat of every tree of the garden?" (Genesis 3:1). And the woman affirmed that it was so: "We may eat of the fruit of the trees of the garden: But of the fruit of the tree which is in the midst of the garden, God hath said, Ye shall not eat of it, neither shall ye touch it, lest ye die."

The serpent's reply is scornful: "Ye shall not surely die," he said. "For God doth know that in the day ye eat thereof, then your eyes shall be opened, and ye shall be as gods, *knowing good and evil.*" The serpent was wrong. They would not die immediately, but they would die. The rest of what the serpent said turns out to be true. Their eyes were opened; they became aware of things that heretofore they had not seen. Things that had before seemed insignificant now took on new meaning to them.

We have to pause at this point to clarify a couple of things. First, the Hebrew word translated "evil" does not denote malicious evil, but mere adversity. Properly, it is the tree of the knowledge of "good and bad." (In modern usage, evil means "morally reprehensible." In the Bible, evil means "adversity," or the opposite of good.)

Second, the word "knowledge" means "to ascertain by seeing." In other words, it implies *experiencing* something, not merely knowing about it. Thus, "Adam *knew* his wife and she conceived." The knowledge of good and evil meant that man would see good and see adversity, in the sense of *experiencing* it. Life would now have an upside and a downside. He would be living in a very different world.

Nearly everything that troubles us about God and about life depends on our understanding this simple truth. Adam had a choice of two worlds. One where he would know nothing but good, and the other where he would know good and bad.

Some have said the trees are symbolic of two ways of living. Others have thought that man fell when he ate of the wrong tree and his nature was changed. But the trees seem rather to symbolize two environments in which man might live. It wasn't man's *nature* that was changed when he sinned. It was his environment. He went from an environment that offered nothing but good things to an environment that offered both good and bad. Consider the consequences of the choice. Here is what God said to Adam:

> *Because you listened to your wife and ate from the tree about which I commanded you, 'You must not eat of it,' Cursed is the ground because of you; through painful toil you will eat of it all the days of your life. It will produce thorns and thistles for you, and you will eat the plants of the field. By the sweat of your brow you will eat your food until you return to the ground, since from it you were taken; for dust you are and to dust you will return (Genesis 3:17-19).*

It was not *man* who was cursed. It was the *ground*. God did not tell Adam, "You will be different." Rather he told him that his *environment* would be different. These are *consequences* of his choice, rather than punishments for having made it. Adam was dirt and would have, in the normal course of events returned to dirt. It would have been the Tree of Life that made it different and he was now isolated from that tree. No longer could he eat of the fruit of the trees there. Now he would eat the plants of the field.

This may explain the fate of the woman as well. To the woman, God said: "I will greatly increase your pains in childbearing; with pain you will give birth to children. Your desire will be for your husband, and he will rule over you." This certainly sounds like a change in the physical nature of woman, but it may be only a figure of speech. It was certain that the woman would be away from the Tree of Life. She would no longer have access to *the healing leaves* of that tree.

As a consequence of isolation from Eden, the health of the man and woman would deteriorate and the labor and pain of childbirth would be much worse. It may have been more a consequence of isolation than a curse from God. And, in the wild environment outside of Eden, the superior strength of the man would become a telling difference between the two. Even their relationship would change. And so it was that:

> *The LORD God made garments of skin for Adam and his wife and clothed them. And the LORD God said, 'The man has now become like one of us, knowing good and evil. He must not be allowed to reach out his hand and take also from the tree of life and eat, and live forever.' So the LORD God banished him from the Garden of Eden to work the ground from which he had been taken. After he drove the man out, he placed on the east side of the Garden of Eden cherubim and a flaming sword flashing back and forth to guard the way to the tree of life (Genesis 3:21-24).*

Why clothes? Because they would now face a hostile environment. They were banished from the Garden. They and their children would face that flaming sword every time they thought of returning to the garden.

There is one other thing in this passage that must not be overlooked. The serpent was right when he said: "ye shall be as gods, *knowing good and evil.*" For God himself said, "The man has now become like one of us, knowing good and evil." Does God know evil? Of course He does. He had long since had to deal with the Adversary, the one we know as Satan. At some point in the history of the planet, there had been war between God and Satan, apparently more than once.[iv]

The Garden of Eden was a little sanctuary in a dangerous world where adversity walked. Adam was free and he made the choice of a free man to live in the world where God *and* the Devil both lived and worked. Adam was free himself to do good or to do evil, for if a man is not free to do evil, he is not free. If a man is not free to suffer the consequences of his actions, he is not free. If a man is not free to hurt other men, he is not free.

One of the terrible things to come from Adam's choice is that we are all now subject to the consequences of the choices of others. Countless millions have died in useless wars because some man wanted power over other men. Millions died in Hitler's concentration camps, because of the choices made by one demented man and his evil lieutenants.

But God did not choose evil for man. Man himself made that choice long ago. And the sobering truth is, when we have been given the same choice, we have made the same decision. It doesn't really help to blame Adam for what we ourselves have done.

But are we forever stuck with that choice? Is there any way we can go back to that idyllic world of Eden with access to a healing tree, to health, to safety? Is there no bridge to that world? Well, yes and no. There is a bridge back across to that world, but it lies ahead of us.

I must now change the scene and the metaphor. Jesus is confronted by a crowd of uncommitted followers. He had given all of them a free meal and they seem still to be preoccupied with that. They had bread on the mind, so bread is the metaphor of choice. "Our fathers did eat manna in the desert," they said, "as it is written, He gave them bread from heaven to eat" (John 6:31). They seem to be aware of the miraculous nature of the meal they had just eaten and they were looking for an explanation.

"I will tell you the truth, then," Jesus said. "Moses gave you not that bread from heaven; but my Father giveth you the true bread from heaven. For the bread of God is he which cometh down from heaven, and giveth life unto the world." First we were talking about a tree that gives life, now it is bread that gives life.

"I am the living bread which came down from heaven," Jesus continued, "if any man eat of this bread, he shall live for ever: and the bread that I will give is my flesh, which I will give for the life of the world." Adam and Eve might have eaten of the Tree of Life and lived forever. Now Jesus says that his flesh is the bread which makes it possible to live forever: "Verily, verily, I say unto you, Except ye eat the flesh of the Son of man, and drink his blood, ye have no life in you. Whoso eateth my flesh, and drinketh my blood, hath eternal life; and I will raise him up at the last day" (John 6:53-54).

In a manner of speaking, Jesus is the bridge back to the world Adam and Eve left. He gives us the choice again. As He told doubting Thomas: "I am the way, the truth, and the life." The way where? To the Tree of Life.

Recently, a friend asked me a question about the Tree of Life that I had not considered before. He wondered if the Tree of Life was a one shot thing (eat of it and live forever), or if it was something Adam had to continue to eat of in order to live. I hadn't thought of it in those terms, but perhaps it's time we did.

The events in Eden do not suggest that eating of the Tree of Life would make Adam a spirit being. What if the Tree of Life and the other trees in the Garden were the ongoing source of life in the flesh? Consider Jesus' ministry in the flesh. A woman with an issue of blood for 12 years comes up behind Jesus in a press of people. She touches the hem of his garment and is made whole on the spot. What changed *spiritually*? The text has nothing to say about that. She was already a woman of faith, a believer. She said that if she could just touch the hem of his garment, she would be made whole. And after she touched him, *"she felt in her body that she was healed of that plague" (Mark 5:29)*. As far as we know, the woman lived on, grew old and died. She wasn't given eternal life. She was simply given life. What is the difference? *Eternal* life doesn't end; her life did.

Then there is the man Jesus encountered in the synagogue with a withered hand. Jesus healed him instantly, but there isn't a hint that anything else was changed. He healed a man born blind, and another who had been lame from birth, two major birth defects. But what changed spiritually? As far as we know, nothing. Even the most remarkable example in the New Testament of the giving of life, the raising of Lazarus from the dead, only gave Lazarus *temporal* life. The gift of eternal life in the spirit would require something more.

All this deepens the mystery. Why did healing figure so prominently in Jesus' ministry if it played no role in "spiritual" salvation? Part of the answer is found in the Last Supper. For our purpose here, the best account is Paul's instructions to the Corinthians regarding this most important of Christian observances.

> *For I have received of the Lord that which also I delivered unto you,* " *Paul said,* "*that the Lord Jesus the same night in which he was betrayed took bread: And when he had given thanks, he brake it, and said, Take, eat: this is my body, which is broken for you: this do in remembrance of me (1 Corinthians 11:23-24).*

Every Christian is familiar with these words, and especially with the words that follow: "After the same manner also he took the cup, when he had supped, saying, This cup is the new testament in my blood: this do ye, as oft as ye drink it, in remembrance of me. For as often as ye eat this bread, and drink this cup, ye do show the Lord's death till he come."

Now here was my problem. I grew up very familiar with the idea of Jesus' blood sacrifice. The hymnals of every church I attended were replete with songs about the blood of Jesus and its power over sin. I knew I had been forgiven by the shed blood of Christ. I had sung, "There's Power in the Blood," and "There is a fountain filled with blood." I observed Communion with tears on my cheeks more than once as a young man. I knew I was a sinner and I knew that Jesus shed his blood for me.

But year after year I ate the bread at the Lord's Supper without a second thought. I never asked why the bread was there. Why not the cup alone? It was a long time before the remainder of Paul's instructions came home to me.

> *"Wherefore whosoever shall eat this bread, and drink this cup of the Lord, unworthily,* " *said Paul,* "*shall be guilty of the body and blood of the Lord. But let a man examine himself, and so let him eat of that bread, and drink of that cup. For he that eateth and drinketh unworthily, eateth and drinketh damnation to himself,* **not discerning the Lord's body.** *For this cause many are weak and sickly among you, and many sleep" (1 Corinthians 11:27-30).*

I never thought of taking Communion unworthily, but I found a perfect description of myself in the phrase, "not discerning the Lord's body." Then I saw that Paul connects the idea of ignoring the Lord's body to weakness, sickness and death, three things that the flesh of Christ can cure.

Why did Jesus heal so many sick people? "Because he could," is not good enough. Neither is compassion an explanation for why he did what he did. Jesus always had compassion, but he did not always heal. On one occasion, he refused to heal a woman's daughter at first and only relented in the face of her great faith. [v] In the towns where he grew up, Jesus was not able to do very many miracles in the face of the unbelief of the people. [vi]

Jesus seems to have answered this question in one of the more remarkable instances of healing in his ministry. He was in his own city at the time, a place where relatively few believed on him. While he was teaching in a house, some men brought a friend in the hope he could be healed. He was a paralytic and had to be carried on a bed. They couldn't get to Jesus because of the crush, so they went up on the roof, broke open a hole, and let their friend down on ropes in front of Jesus. He, seeing their faith, said to the poor man before him, "Take heart, son; *your sins are forgiven*" (Matthew 9:2 NIV).

Some of the sages, the law teachers, were sitting there and concluded without saying so that Jesus was blasphemous. Only God could forgive sins. But Jesus knew what they were thinking and addressed the issue: "Why do you entertain evil thoughts in your hearts? Which is easier: to say, 'Your sins are forgiven,' or to say, 'Get up and walk'? But so that you may know that the Son of Man has authority on earth to forgive sins. . ." Then he said to the paralytic, "Get up, take your mat and go home."

Jesus, then, had the power to forgive sins. His healing of all manner of sickness and disease was evidence of that power. And we can't escape the realization that there is a connection between the forgiveness of sins and healing of the body. Peter recognized this when he spoke of Christ's sacrifice of his body: "Who his own self bare our sins in his own body on the tree, that we, being dead to sins, should live unto righteousness: *by whose stripes ye were healed*" (1 Peter 2:24).

He bore our sins in his body. We are healed by his stripes.

There was more to the sacrifice of Christ than shedding his blood. Peter draws these ideas from the Prophet Isaiah who said of the suffering Messiah:

> *Surely he has borne our infirmities and carried our diseases; yet we accounted him stricken, struck down by God, and afflicted. But he was wounded for our transgressions, crushed for our iniquities; upon him was the punishment that made us whole, and by his bruises we are healed (Isaiah 53:4-5 NRSV).*

Once again, the metaphor will change. The Tree of Life has become the Body of Christ. Now, the Body of Christ will become the Tree of Life. Late in the book of Revelation, we find John nearing the end of an incredible experience. He has seen vision after vision and heard words it is not lawful for a man to utter. He is about to see something that still boggles the mind after 2,000 years. "And I saw a new heaven and a new earth: for the first heaven and the first earth were passed away; and there was no more sea" (Revelation 21:1).

We must not forget that John is in vision. What John is describing is not actual events, but a vision representing things and events, some completely beyond our ability to see. What John sees is physically impossible. It is surely spiritual, and symbolic, but that does not make it any less real. John continues to describe what he saw. It is like a dream.

> *And I John saw the holy city, new Jerusalem, coming down from God out of heaven, prepared as a bride adorned for her husband. And I heard a great voice out of heaven saying, Behold, the tabernacle of God is with men, and he will dwell with them, and they shall be his people, and God himself shall be with them, and be their God. And God shall wipe away all tears from their eyes; and there shall be no more death, neither sorrow, nor crying, neither shall there be any more pain: for the former things are passed away. And he that sat upon the throne said, Behold, I make all things new. And he said unto me, Write: for these words are true and faithful (Revelation 21:2-5).*

"Behold, I make all things new." Man is getting a clean slate. All the exposure to evil that arose from the choice made by Adam and Eve is now reversed. Remember what God told Adam as he left the garden: "cursed is the ground for thy sake; in sorrow shalt thou eat of it all the days of thy life." Now there will be no more sorrow. And remember what God told Eve as she left: "I will greatly increase your pains in childbearing; with pain you will give birth to children." Now there will be no more pain. Even more important, there will be no more death.

The holy city, New Jerusalem, appears to be the Tabernacle of God, his dwelling place. And now he will dwell among men. Now he identifies himself.

And he said unto me, It is done. I am Alpha and Omega, the beginning and the end. I will give unto him that is athirst of the fountain of the water of life freely. He that overcometh shall inherit all things; and I will be his God, and he shall be my son. But the fearful, and unbelieving, and the abominable, and murderers, and whoremongers, and sorcerers, and idolaters, and all liars, shall have their part in the lake which burneth with fire and brimstone: which is the second death (Revelation 21:6-8).

God seems to think nothing of mixing his metaphors. We go from the Tree of Life, to the Body of Christ, to the fountain of the water of life, and we still aren't finished. Now an angel comes to show John "the bride, the Lamb's wife." We must not forget that this is a vision and heavy with symbolism. The angel carries John away to a great, high mountain and shows him the city. It defies description, but John tries anyway. The gates are each one a pearl. All the foundations are precious stones. And the city does not merely reflect light, it glistens with a light of its own. One thing that reminds us that it is a dream is the size of the city. It lies 1500 miles on a side and 1500 miles high. The space shuttle only goes up 200 miles. It is physically impossible, but in a dream, anything can work. [vii]

The message that comes with the vision brings an unexpected image. This is after the destruction of the old earth and the creation of

47

a new heaven and a new earth. And yet there is an inside and an outside. Just as the Garden of Eden was not the whole world, neither is this city.

> *And I saw no temple therein: for the Lord God Almighty and the Lamb are the temple of it. And the city had no need of the sun, neither of the moon, to shine in it: for the glory of God did lighten it, and the Lamb is the light thereof. And the nations of them which are saved shall walk in the light of it: and the kings of the earth do bring their glory and honour into it. And the gates of it shall not be shut at all by day: for there shall be no night there. And they shall bring the glory and honour of the nations into it. And there shall in no wise enter into it any thing that defileth, neither whatsoever worketh abomination, or maketh a lie: but they which are written in the Lamb's book of life (Revelation 21:22-27).*

In the vision, there is movement into the city. There are qualifications for inclusion and conditions for exclusion. Then the angel shows John something that brings the Bible full circle.

> *And he showed me a pure river of water of life, clear as crystal, proceeding out of the throne of God and of the Lamb. In the midst of the street of it, and on either side of the river, was there the tree of life, which bare twelve manner of fruits, and yielded her fruit every month: and the leaves of the tree were for the healing of the nations (Revelation 22:1,2).*

I recall the first time I read this. I wondered how a tree could be on both sides of a river. Then I realized that the Tree of Life is not a single tree but a *kind* of tree. Here, there are twelve varieties of the tree with twelve varieties of fruit. (What's more, there is a moon, for without a moon there are no months.)

I think it was the leaves of the tree that caused my friend to ask me if the Tree of Life in the Garden of Eden was a one shot deal, eat it once and live forever, or if it was something one had to eat again and again to maintain life, to restore life, to heal the decaying human body.

I don't know that I can answer that question, but it does seem that the Bible begins and ends with the Tree of Life. And that the Tree of Life is somehow linked to Christ. Then when Johns says, "And there shall be no more curse," it is once again to undo the damage of the choice made in the Garden of Eden. For when Adam was expelled, God said, "Cursed is the ground because of you." The angel then began to close the message to John, saying:

> *Seal not the sayings of the prophecy of this book: for the time is at hand. He that is unjust, let him be unjust still: and he which is filthy, let him be filthy still: and he that is righteous, let him be righteous still: and he that is holy, let him be holy still. And, behold, I come quickly; and my reward is with me, to give every man according as his work shall be. I am Alpha and Omega, the beginning and the end, the first and the last (Revelation 22:10-13).*

It is perhaps not so strange that the Tree of Life was there at the beginning and the end of the Bible story. Since the tree seems clearly to represent the eternal life that is in Christ. Man started in the Garden of Eden with a choice. He ends in the City of God, once again with a choice.

> *Blessed are they that do his commandments, that they may have right to the tree of life, and may enter in through the gates into the city. For without are dogs, and sorcerers, and whoremongers, and murderers, and idolaters, and whosoever loveth and maketh a lie (Revelation 22:14-15).*

Over the years I have been asked repeatedly about this verse, how there could be any of these people left? Remember, this is a vision, and what it has done is to bring the Bible full circle. We started with the Garden of Eden and two people. Now we have a city with an innumerable multitude of people. We started with a safe place, a world with no downside, but with a gate to the other world outside. We end with a safe place and twelve gates that are closed to the world outside. We have the tree of life in twelve varieties. We have trees for the healing of the races. Man has been restored to the world he once left. We no longer have to live with the results of Adam's choice.

What I here call, "the choice," theologians have long called, "the fall." There are more questions about this event than I can answer, but it seems evident that, on that day, mankind lost everything we today wish we had.

---

i. (Revelation 22:2) "In the midst of the street of it, and on either side of the river, was there the tree of life, which bare twelve manner of fruits, and yielded her fruit every month: and the leaves of the tree were for the healing of the nations." The word for nations is the Greek *ethnos* which is used commonly in the New Testament for Gentiles. The word actually denotes a race of people in the singular. Used in the plural it means "The Peoples" in the sense of the nations. Jews used the term to refer to nations not Jewish, but the Bible seems to include everyone.

ii. Clothes are not merely for the sake of modesty. They are protective. Adam and Eve needed no protection from this environment.

iii. Genesis 2:16-17.

iv. See Revelation 12:7; 13:7; 19:11; Ephesians 6:12. While the references in Revelation seem to be future, the adversarial relationship between God and the Devil certainly predated man.

v. Matthew 15:22-28.

vi. Mark 6:4-6.

vii. Revelation 21:9 ff.

7

The World We Want

Therefore the LORD God sent him forth from the garden of Eden,
to till the ground from whence he was taken.
So he drove out the man;
and he placed at the east of the garden of Eden Cherubims,
and a flaming sword which turned every way,
to keep the way of the tree of life. (Genesis 3:23-24)

Out of any great disaster, God is questioned anew. How could a God who is good allow such suffering when it is in his hand to prevent it? One of the outcomes of such disaster is often a curious mishmash of half-baked theologies. There is a term for the problem: *theodicy*, "the defense of God's goodness and omnipotence in view of the existence of evil."

David Hart, writing in the March, 2005 issue of "First Things" acknowledged that it was human "to feel some measure of spontaneous resentment toward God," or whatever other force might have been at work when disaster strikes. More than once in my life I have had to console a person who simply could not understand how God could allow bad things in his world. He is all powerful, isn't he? He is good, isn't he? Then how could he let this happen?

It might have been a third of a million people wiped out in a disaster, or thirty kids killed in a school bus accident, but the questions are all the same. "Why did the terrible tsunami in Southeast

Asia take so much innocent life?" For even though you might believe that some of those who perished were terrible sinners, most of them were just like you. Or were children.

Why did the tsunami take so much life? The answer to the question is utterly simple. A section of the earth's crust shifted creating an earthquake and an upthrust that created a tidal wave that swept toward distant coastlines at the speed of a jet aircraft. People were swept away like ants on your sidewalk are swept away when you spray them with a garden hose.

That's all, nothing complicated. The world is a dangerous place. Bad things happen in dangerous places. But that doesn't answer the question entirely, does it? Why didn't God make a better world, a less dangerous world? He could have done it that way, couldn't he? Truth is, we have to believe that God created the best of all possible worlds. So how do we explain this world in that light?

It's not easy, but let me lay out an alternative for us to consider. I am sure you have heard of gravity. Gravity is not a law. It is a *property of matter*. Objects that have mass attract other objects that have mass. Gravity is essential to an ordered universe. Gravity is essential to keeping you in your chair. Gravity is a weak force. It exists between you and the person sitting next to you, but it is so weak you cannot feel it. It is only when objects become huge that gravity becomes an important force. And even though we cannot feel it, gravity is transmitted across light years of space, to cause galaxies to spiral, and to create the heavens in the relationships we can see in the night sky.

For all that we see around us to work, the earth has to be a fairly precise size. It has to have sufficient mass to hold us on the surface without crushing us, to hold the moon in place to create the tides and influence the weather. It has to be the right size, traveling at the right speed, attracted by the sun which has to be the right size to hold us in orbit and to provide the energy we need. All these things have to be just so in order for life as we know it to exist.

But there are consequences that go with the properties of this design. The mass of the earth is such that it creates enormous pressures at the center, pressures which create a molten core. The properties of matter create this naturally. The result is that the crust of the earth floats on a sea of molten lava. Which, in itself is a source of energy. But, the earth moves beneath our feet, and we don't like that very much. There are times and places where it can kill us.

The Garden of Eden was not one of those places. If Adam and Eve had felt an earthquake, it would have been scary for a moment. But there were no houses to fall on them, and the shaking of the trees would only have dropped fruit on the ground which might have been downright convenient. But there were dangerous places on the earth, even then.

Those dangers were not evil. They merely arose from the properties of matter. And the Garden of Eden was a safe place within an otherwise dangerous world. Earthquakes and volcanoes were not dangerous there. There were no thorns, no briars, no poison ivy.

And they were both naked, the man and his wife,
and were not ashamed (Genesis 2:25).

I want to suggest a different view of what happened in Eden and the consequences of what happened for us. I think it is odd how virtually every version of the Bible chooses shame as the operative emotion in the face of nakedness. "Ashamed" is not the basic meaning of the Hebrew word *buwsh* we find here. The verb means, "to pale," and a simple word study reveals a wide variety of situations that might cause one to turn pale. Consider an alternative which is consistent with the usage of the word *buwsh*: "And they were both naked, the man and his wife, and were not *concerned*." Remember? No thorns, no briars, no poison ivy. No need for clothing for protection from the environment. This is important in view of later developments.

Enter, the serpent. More subtle than any beast of the field, he cajoled Adam and Eve into trying out the fruit of the tree of the knowledge of good and evil. From this simple choice arose the law of unintended consequences: "And the eyes of them both were opened, and they knew that they were naked; and they sewed fig leaves together, and made themselves aprons" (Genesis 3:1-7).

Absolutely nothing had changed in reality, but everything had changed *in their eyes*. There was no reason for them to now be ashamed of their nakedness. But they apparently did begin to feel vulnerable. The idea that they were *embarrassed* at their nakedness doesn't seem to follow, but a sense of vulnerability does.

I recall, years ago, watching a BBC television program on Nudism. They were interviewing people in a nudist colony that was right down the road from the college where I was teaching. The interviewer asked if there was any special care that they had to take. "Oh yes," the woman answered. "The most dangerous thing I do is fry sausage." I think she wore an apron for that activity, but it was certainly not out of embarrassment or shame. After all, she was right there, stark naked on national television. She wore the apron for protection.

Eden was a safe environment, but we can feel very vulnerable, even when we are really quite safe. Now, for what followed.

> *And they heard the voice of the LORD God walking in the garden in the cool of the day: and Adam and his wife hid themselves from the presence of the LORD God amongst the trees of the garden. And the LORD God called unto Adam, and said unto him, Where art thou? And he said, I heard thy voice in the garden, and I was afraid, because I was naked; and I hid myself (Genesis 3:8-10).*

Now if we take this in the traditional view of shame, God's reply is almost laughable. He said, "Who told you that you were naked?" We don't know how long Adam and Eve had cavorted around the garden naked. They didn't have mirrors, but they sure had hands and eyes. Their nakedness was no surprise to them, but their vulnerability may have been.

"Hast thou eaten of the tree," God asked, "whereof I commanded thee that thou shouldest not eat?" Now the finger pointing begins. Adam blames Eve, Eve blames the snake. Finally, God cuts to the chase. He begins to explain to the first couple the consequences of what they had done: *"Unto the woman he said, I will greatly multiply thy sorrow and thy conception; in sorrow thou shalt bring forth children; and thy desire shall be to thy husband, and he shall rule over thee" (Genesis 3:16).*

Traditional theology holds that this sorrow and pain in

childbearing is a curse on the woman, as though she had changed anatomically. But what if that is not the case? What if this is merely the consequences of being isolated from the Tree of Life or other trees that were there for healing, that might have made childbirth easy, painless and safe?

> *And unto Adam he said, Because thou hast hearkened unto the voice of thy wife, and hast eaten of the tree, of which I commanded thee, saying, Thou shalt not eat of it: cursed is the ground for thy sake; in sorrow shalt thou eat of it all the days of thy life; Thorns also and thistles shall it bring forth to thee; and thou shalt eat the herb of the field; In the sweat of thy face shalt thou eat bread, till thou return unto the ground; for out of it wast thou taken: for dust thou art, and unto dust shalt thou return (vv. 17-19).*

Note well: it was not Adam who was changed. It was the ground. And the ground was changed because he could not stay in the garden. He had to leave the safe place, the easy place, the world we all want. It was his environment that was changed, not his nature. And, because their environment would be changed, "Unto Adam also and to his wife did the LORD God make coats of skins, and clothed them."

Applying the simple, obvious explanation, none of this had anything to do with sex or shame. It was because the environment would no longer be safe or friendly. They were too vulnerable to be left unclothed.

> *Therefore the LORD God sent him forth from the garden of Eden, to till the ground from whence he was taken. So he drove out the man; and he placed at the east of the garden of Eden Cherubims, and a flaming sword which turned every way, to keep the way of the tree of life (v. 24).*

And all mankind ever since has been subject to earthquakes, volcanos, tornados, hurricanes, tsunamis, and to the stupidity and violence perpetrated by other men. Now, we live with a lot of bad things in our lives. Addressing these things Jesus made this observation:

> *There were present at that season some that told him of the Galilaeans, whose blood Pilate had mingled with their sacrifices. And Jesus answering said unto them, Suppose ye that these Galilaeans were sinners above all the Galilaeans, because they suffered such things? I tell you, Nay: but, except ye repent, ye shall all likewise perish. Or those eighteen, upon whom the tower in Siloam fell, and slew them, think ye that they were sinners above all men that dwelt in Jerusalem? I tell you, Nay: but, except ye repent, ye shall all likewise perish (Luke 13:1-5).*

There are two sources of bad things described here. Accidents, either of nature or human failure, and the wicked acts of wicked men. Neither should be blamed on God. We should accept responsibility ourselves. We could, of course, blame it on Adam and Eve, but I have a feeling that, given the same choice, we would have done the same thing.

The answer to the question of *theodicy* is simple enough. God is good. He made man free. He made the best of all possible worlds for man to live in, but he gave us a choice of two. He did this because we were not to be specimens in a zoo. He wanted us to be human, made in the image of God.

We aren't terribly happy with the world God has made for us. Couldn't he have made a world that had no downside to it? Actually, he did. We call it the Garden of Eden. But did he have to create that dangerous world outside? I don't know. But it isn't dangerous to God and it wasn't dangerous to Adam and Eve until they got bored with the safety of Eden.

We aren't terribly happy with the way God made us either. It is not uncommon to get a letter from someone asking why God didn't make man so he could not sin. Actually, God could and did make creatures that cannot sin. We call them cows. Is that what we want to be?

We think we want a different world. We don't like the one God made. But, the world we want is the world we left.

8

Liberty

Then the serpent said to the woman,
"You will not surely die.
For God knows that in the day you eat of it
your eyes will be opened, and you will be like God,
knowing good and evil" (Genesis 3:4-5 NKJV).

It must have been a hard decision for God to make. I don't mean to suggest that anything is really hard for God, but the decision had consequences that even God could not have treated lightly. The decision to put the tree of the knowledge of good and evil in the Garden of Eden had consequences for all of history. By putting that tree there, God effectively created a gate out of the Garden of Eden. He gave man a choice about the kind of a world that he would live in. If Paradise became boring for man, he had an alternative.

God (1) told Adam and Eve not to eat of the tree, but (2) left them free to eat it anyway. Much is contained in these two simple facts. But there was more. In order for God to achieve his objective, it was necessary that man be free. But that idea has terrible consequences. If man is not free to do evil, for example, he is not free. If he is not free to hurt other people, he's not free. If man is not free to suffer, then he's not free. If the innocent are not free to suffer at the hands of evil men, then they are not free.

Liberty has consequences. Man wants freedom, and at the same time he wants to be free from the consequences of his actions.

These two wants simply cannot be reconciled.

Why is evil allowed in God's good world if God is good? The answer is utterly simple: God is good, man is free. And if you're not free to do evil, you're not free at all.

It might have been possible for God to create a world where man would never harm innocent children. But that world would not have been free. In order to be free ourselves we must be free to suffer the consequences of the choices of other people. If a burglar makes a choice to break into your home, you suffer the loss of your goods or your property because of a choice that he made. He was free to make that choice. If he hadn't been free to make it, he's not free at all. And if you hadn't been free to suffer it, you wouldn't be free at all.

Every intervention of God in the affairs of men is an abridgment of the freedom he intended for man. If you pray and ask God to help you find a job, you are asking God to abridge the freedom of the person who does the hiring. Not only that, but you are asking him to deny the job to someone else who may have been better qualified. Now I believe God may do that for people, but let's not overlook what it costs.

In order to put food on the table for your hungry children, God may have to abridge your freedom to be poor. If God actually intervenes, if he has to do something to give food to your children that you otherwise could not provide, he is abridging your freedom to be poor and hungry. It's a freedom you have that comes right along with your freedom to avoid work. It comes right along with your freedom to be feckless in the use of your money. It comes right along with the freedom to overcharge your credit cards to the point that you can't afford the things that you need to buy for your children. All these freedoms are ours. We can do what we wish, and that means that our children are free to suffer the consequences of our decisions as well.

Man is conflicted about freedom. Freedom is good, but we will lay it down in a heartbeat once it becomes too heavy to bear. We are tempted to lay our freedom down if someone offers us food, shelter and clothing. People have actually accepted slavery in order to fill their empty bellies and to get a kind of security from those who would do them harm. History is full of stories like this.

And so God, in his law, made provision for the renewal of

liberty after it had been laid down. Every seven years, there was a clearing of the debts. The land was to lie fallow that year, all debts were canceled and *all slaves set free*. At the end of 49 years, in the 50th year, a liberty was proclaimed throughout the land. [i]

Liberty is a marvelous word. What it meant to the Israelites was that all the stupid things they had done that got them into trouble were swept off the table. They got a clean start. In effect, it probably was of more benefit to the children of those who had lost their liberty. If your dad had sold off the family inheritance because of profligate spending, it came back to you in the 50th year.

That year was called a Jubilee. [ii] The Israelites were not to sow a crop in that year, nor were they to reap that which grew of itself. It was holy. They could eat it, but they could not make a cash crop with it. They were to allow the poor to come and get what they needed to eat in that year.

In the passage describing the Jubilee, Moses explains how a piece of property could be sold. The price was reckoned according to the number of years to the Jubilee. It was, in effect, a leasehold sale.

There are some interesting consequences that flow from this. For one thing, all land titles flew right out the window. Family trees were important because the title reverted to the first heir in line. You didn't plant in that year because the land might no longer be yours. You didn't harvest because you may not have been the one who made the initial investments. Since the owners of all crops were in transition, the crops were thrown open to everyone to eat what he liked.

When I lived in England, I learned that much of the land belonged to the Crown. You could buy that land as a leasehold, but only for a specified number of years. After that, the property returned to the Crown. Land not subject to this restriction could be sold freehold, that is, it could be held in perpetuity.

The land in Israel was deemed to be owned by God and a fifty year leasehold was granted to the tribes by inheritance. At the end of every fifty years, the property reverted to the heir of the man who received the lot from God.

Twice in this law, there is a warning against oppression. It was considered oppression to try to hold on to the property beyond the Jubilee year. Much of the oppression men suffer in this world is self-inflicted. It comes about by the foolish things that we do. The law of Moses, for example, made provision for punishing a thief. He had to make restitution plus penalties. If he couldn't pay what was required, he was sold as a slave. But an Israelite could not be sold as a slave in perpetuity. He could not be held for more than six years, and then he had to be released – he got a fresh start. At the Jubilee, they even got their land back.

And of course throughout the Bible God repeatedly tells Israel, "I want you to think very carefully about this because you're strangers and sojourners with me and you better be careful how you treat the people who are strangers and sojourners with you. Realizing that just as I am treating you, you need to be careful to treat those people well." [iii]

There's an interesting illustration or example of these laws in the Book of Jeremiah. [iv] It is not entirely clear what happened, but it seems that King Zedekiah and all the nobles and princes had cut a deal to let all their Hebrew servants go free. They were allowed to retain a non-Hebrew slave. The idea was that no man should serve himself of his brother.

The deal was put into effect, and it was probably in a year of release that this happened. Hebrew servants were treated as contracted servants. The contract had an expiration date, and when the time of the contract was up, they let them go.

In Jeremiah's account of this, we aren't told how long it took, but before long, the princes began making these same people servants and handmaids again. So the word of God came to Jeremiah with a message:

> *This is what the LORD, the God of Israel, says: I made a covenant with your forefathers when I brought them out of Egypt, out of the land of slavery. I said, 'Every seventh year each of you must free any fellow Hebrew who has sold himself to you. After he has served you six years, you must let him go free.' Your fathers, however, did not listen to me or pay attention to me. Recently you repented and did what is right in my sight: Each of you proclaimed freedom to his countrymen. You even made a covenant before me*

in the house that bears my Name (Jeremiah 34:13-15 NIV).

Mind you, the people who were in slavery were there for a reason. They were often miscreants. They had done stupid things, they had been criminals, they had gone into debt, they had done things that had led to them being made slaves in the first place. Nevertheless, they weren't slaves for life. They had to be let go. The problem arose when those princes who had become accustomed to free labor now had to pay for it. So they broke their covenant.

> *But now you have turned around and profaned my name; each of you has taken back the male and female slaves you had set free to go where they wished. You have forced them to become your slaves again. Therefore, this is what the LORD says: You have not obeyed me; you have not proclaimed freedom for your fellow countrymen. So I now proclaim 'freedom' for you, declares the LORD – 'freedom' to fall by the sword, plague and famine. I will make you abhorrent to all the kingdoms of the earth (vv. 16-17).*

These are not slaves of a conquered country, by the way. They were supposed to be contractual servants of their own people. But the contract had been broken.

What Jeremiah is telling them is this. Since they were not willing to accept the liberty defined by the law, they would be granted *complete* freedom. They would be free from God's blessings and protection, free to suffer whatever evil the world had in store for them.

And this is the reason we have so many terrible things in our lives. It is because we have made choices that have brought them our way. We have made choices that have taken us out of the road that God wanted us to walk. We have made choices that have brought bad things upon us, our own sins have opened the door for these things to come upon us.

We have exercised our freedom, and God has granted to us a

liberty, a liberty to the pain, destruction and loss that sin brings with it.

Freedom is a heavy burden to be borne. It is sad to say that some people, freed from servitude, want to go back. Just as Israel, freed from the slavery of Egypt wanted to go back, some men who have been freed from jail want to return. Men have actually committed crimes in order to get back into prison where they were fed and clothed, where they knew the routine and how to live. They have become so institutionalized that they can't live well outside. And so they go out and do the same things that they did before, and back inside they go again.

There are some on the outside who are of the same mind. They want to be taken care of, they want to lay their freedom down, they *want* to be slaves. They want to be servants because then, someone else can take care of them.

Freedom, after all, is a terrible burden. I know it must be, because we complain about it so much. We have a litany of complaints that, at their base, are complaints about freedom. We ask, "Why does God allow war?" That's a complaint about our freedom. "Why does he allow innocent children to suffer?" That also is a complaint about our freedom. "Why did God allow the Holocaust?" Well that's a complaint against the freedom of both Nazis and Jews.

We have the freedom to do good. We have the freedom to hurt. We have the freedom to harm, and if we have it, so do others. If others have that freedom we have the freedom to suffer from what they do. Freedom is a terrible word. It's a frightening word, a dangerous word. And when you understand it, it is the freedom of the tree of the knowledge of good and evil. Remember that the way the Bible uses the word "knowledge" in Genesis refers to the *experiencing* of good and evil.

Adam and Eve made the choice of experiencing good and evil, and we have been living with that choice ever since. Man was told what to do and left free not to do it. He was told what not to do and left free to do it anyway. That's what freedom is. But we want *selective* freedom, we want to be free to do what we want to do, but not free enough to experience the consequences of what we have done.

The irony of it all is that as we exercise our freedom to

choose, what we choose leads us back into bondage again and again and again. And this is why in His original law, God made provision for freeing people. For some people, it required freeing them again and again. In a lifetime, some people could have managed to be slaves and free every seven years. In the same way, some people today are in and out of prison time after time. In every generation, there are people who just can't seem to keep their life together. It may not lead to prison, but each, in his own way, goes back into bondage again and again.

There was a day early in Jesus' ministry when he made a special visit to a synagogue. It appears to be the first sermon of his ministry, because it takes place almost immediately after his temptation by the Devil. As he began to preach, the world begins to learn what Jesus is all about.

> *He came to Nazareth where He had been brought up, and as His custom was He went into the synagogue on the Sabbath day and He stood up for to read. And there was delivered to Him the book of the prophet Isaiah. And when He had opened the book He found the place where it was written, the spirit of the Lord is upon me because He has anointed me to preach the gospel to the poor. He has sent me to heal the brokenhearted, to preach deliverance to the captives, the recovering of sight to the blind, to set at liberty them that are bruised, to preach the acceptable year of the Lord (Luke 4:16-18).*

There is no mistaking what he is talking about. It is a reference to the Jubilee year described here. Jesus sat down and closed the book. Everybody was looking at him, and he said. "This day is this Scripture fulfilled in your ears."

What makes this saying so important is the ease with which man lays down the burden of freedom, the ease with which he enslaves himself again and again. And the terrible price that has to be paid to purchase his freedom again. This is where Jesus begins to reveal that he is the Redeemer, the Savior, the one who bridges the chasm that Adam crossed so very long ago. Jesus is the bridge back to the Tree of Life which Adam lost.

But Jesus was not citing Leviticus in his sermon on that day. Rather he was citing a passage from Isaiah. The remainder of the passage Jesus cited on that day would have been familiar to his audience. The words after "to proclaim the acceptable year of the Lord," are "and the day of the vengeance of our God" (Isaiah 61:2).

What Jesus was doing was preparing the way and making possible what the remainder of that passage said about the work that Jesus would finally do.

> *To comfort all who mourn, to appoint to them who mourn in Zion, to give them beauty for ashes, the oil of joy for mourning, the garment of praise for the spirit of heaviness. All the weight of the world that sits on our shoulders he has come to take away. And they shall rebuild the old wastes, they shall raise up the former desolations, they shall repair the waste cities. The desolations of many generations, strangers shall stand and feed your flocks, the sons of the aliens shall be your vine men, your plow men, but you shall be named the priests of the Lord (See Isaiah 61:3-6).*

It is too easy to forget that salvation, in the sense Christians use the term, is a rescue operation. It is a rescue of people who have lost their freedom because of choices they made. And it is all too easy to forget that salvation is not without cost. Jesus was made, for a time, lower than the angels for the suffering of death.

> *For it became him, by whom are all things and for whom are all things, in bringing many sons to glory, to make the captain of their salvation perfect through suffering. For both he that sanctified and he that sanctifies them are all of one, for which sake he is not ashamed to call them brethren. . . For as much then as the children are partakers of flesh and blood, he also himself took part of the same that through death he might destroy him that has the power of death, that is the devil (Hebrews 2:10-14).*

We are so vulnerable in the world. A man can stand out in a wooded area with a rifle and kill a perfect stranger in a parking lot. Two boys can enter a school with weapons and kill their fellow students. They are free to do it, and their fellow students are free to die. What we must understand about this is that it was necessary for Jesus to make himself vulnerable to the same kind of choices that cause us so much suffering.

Jesus came to deliver those, who through fear of death, were all their lifetime subject to bondage. He did not take on himself the nature of angels, but the nature of men. He walked on earth with us. He was one of us, and he had the freedom to make any choice that we choose to make. But because he was free, he was also subject to the choices that other men made every day.

He escaped out of their hands a few times, but then one night there came a time when he had to submit himself to the decisions that other people were going to make about him. They would take away his dignity, his comfort, his freedom from pain, and even his life. To be truly free, he had to submit himself to the choice that Judas made to sell him out. He had to submit himself to men who were going to mock him and humiliate him and make fun of him.

He had to submit himself to the choices of men who placed a crown of thorns on his head. He had to submit himself to men who would slap him on his face and pull his beard off his face. He had to submit himself to men who made the choice to drag him out to Golgotha having scourged him, to crucify him and leave him hanging in the sun to die. These decisions were all made by human beings who made choices to kill the Son of God. And because of our freedom, he accepted the freedom to suffer. When you think of it this way, a passage in Isaiah takes on new importance:

> *He grew up before him like a tender shoot, and like a root out of dry ground. He had no beauty or majesty to attract us to him, nothing in his appearance that we should desire him. He was despised and rejected by men, a man of sorrows, and familiar with suffering. Like one from whom men hide their faces he was despised, and we esteemed him not. Surely he took up our infirmities and carried our sorrows, yet we*

*considered him stricken by God, smitten by him, and
afflicted. But he was pierced for our transgressions,
he was crushed for our iniquities; the punishment that
brought us peace was upon him, and by his wounds
we are healed. We all, like sheep, have gone astray,
each of us has turned to his own way; and the LORD
has laid on him the iniquity of us all (Isaiah 53:2-6).*

Jesus is a high priest who can be touched with the feeling of
our infirmities. He was tempted in every way as we are. He had all
the choices before him that we have to make.[v] Jesus did this
voluntarily. It had to be voluntary for it to mean anything. If the
Father had required it of him, it would not have been a choice freely
made.

Having fought the battle with this choice in the Garden of
Gethsemane, he was able to tell Pilate, "I can say the word and have a
legion of angels take me out of here. You have no power against me
except it were given to you by God." Jesus had a choice right up to
the last.

Freedom is highly problematical for us. We must never forget
that if we are truly to be free, then other people are going to have to
suffer because of the choices that we make. Our freedom to choose
means somebody somewhere can get hurt by the things that we do. If
I'm not free to inflict pain on you, I'm not free. I have the choice to do
it or not. If you're not free to experience that pain, then *you're* not
free.

And what Jesus faced in that long night of his betrayal was
the voluntary subjection to the evil choices of other men. And it's
small wonder that, knowing what was coming, he sweat blood that
night asking if there was some other way to do this thing.

What does all of that mean to us? It is summed up in what
James called, "The Law of Liberty." [vi] For James, this was the Ten
Commandments, but it is perfectly exemplified in the lesson of Adam
and Eve. God told them what not to do, and then left them free to do
it. When you think about it, the Law of God can never be a "yoke of
bondage," because man is always free to do or not do. Even Paul sees
it as a law of liberty: "Stand fast therefore in the *liberty* wherewith
Christ hath made us free, and be not entangled again with the yoke of

bondage" (Galatians 5:1). It is man's laws (the laws of Judaism, in Paul's case) that take away our liberty.

We are always free to obey or disobey and to experience the consequences of that liberty. Freedom carries with it an enormous responsibility.

---

i. Leviticus 25:10.

ii. Leviticus 25:11.

iii. See Exodus 23:9.

iv. See Jeremiah 34.

v. Hebrews 4:14 ff.

vi. James 1:25.

9

Can God Read Your Mind?

The LORD knows the thoughts of man;
he knows that they are futile (Psalm 94:11 NIV).

Can God read your mind? Nearly everyone who believes in God would say yes, God can do anything. He can read your mind. And they could cite the scripture above to prove it.

But if you are a serious Bible reader, you probably have had occasion to wonder if it is quite that simple. There are times when reading the Bible, that we suddenly realize that what we thought we knew about God doesn't work. What made me think about this was an article by Michael Carasik in *Bible Review* titled "Can God Read Minds?" [i]

To even ask the question is to call the issue in doubt, and it is an important issue to say the very least. So why would anyone doubt it? Let me tell you a story from the Bible to illustrate the problem.

Everyone knows the story of Adam and Eve. Placed in the Garden of Eden, they were told they could eat of every tree in the garden except one. If they ate of the tree of the knowledge of good and evil, they would die. [ii]

Enter the serpent. The serpent argued that God was lying. Not only would they not die, but their eyes would be opened to understand all manner of things. Eve listened, looked, tasted, and gave some to Adam to eat. As the serpent had said, their eyes were opened and suddenly, there was a problem with their being naked where there had been no problem before.[iii]

Now where was God when all this was going on? Didn't he know? Isn't God everywhere, all the time? Men throw around terms like omniscient (knows everything) and omnipresent (is everywhere) as though they knew what they were talking about. But why didn't God shout the serpent down when he deceived Eve this way? Surely he could have.

But the plot gets even thicker. Having done this thing they knew they should not have done, they heard the voice of God, walking in the garden and calling out for them: "Where are you." What? God didn't know? Or was he just pretending not to know? Was God dissembling?

Adam answered, "I heard thy voice in the garden, and I was afraid, because I was naked; and I hid myself."

"Who told thee that thou wast naked?" replied God. "Hast thou eaten of the tree, whereof I commanded thee that thou shouldest not eat?" [iv] So did God know or didn't he?

Adam followed through with his excuses and pointed the finger at Eve. "And the LORD God said unto the woman, What is this that thou hast done? And the woman said, The serpent beguiled me, and I did eat."

Now all this could be rhetorical, but it doesn't read that way. It is not just a matter of grabbing a few proof texts to make our point. Rather the whole context sounds like God went away and returned completely unaware of what had happened. You and I may have a different interpretation, but the person who wrote this down had a perspective that is surprising. This is troubling because it seems to limit a God whom we believe has no limits. But if we can keep an open mind, there are other possibilities to consider.

There was, for example, a man named Abraham, elsewhere called "the friend of God." God, along with two angels, came by to visit Abraham on their way to Sodom. Abraham prepared them a meal, and as they were eating, God asked him, "Where is Sarah thy wife?" Abraham replied that she was in the tent.

"When I come to see you next time," the Lord said, "Sarah will have a son" (Genesis 18:10).

Now this might be a startling thing to say to anyone, but both Abraham and Sarah were very old, and well past the time of life to have children. Sarah, standing behind them in the tent heard this and "laughed within herself, saying, After I am waxed old shall I have pleasure, my lord being old also?"

"Why did Sarah laugh," God asked, "saying, Shall I of a surety bear a child, which am old?" So he knew. Perhaps he saw it from her face? Maybe her suppressed laugh was not as suppressed as she thought? Or maybe God read her mind. He went on to ask, "Is any thing too hard for the LORD? At the time appointed I will return unto thee, according to the time of life, and Sarah shall have a son." Sarah tried to deny it, but God wasn't having any of that.

So the men rose up from their meal and turned toward Sodom. Abraham went with them a way down the road. As they walked, God had some things to say to Abraham.

Shall I hide from Abraham that thing which I do; Seeing that Abraham shall surely become a great and mighty nation, and all the nations of the earth shall be blessed in him? For I know him, that he will command his children and his household after him, and they shall keep the way of the LORD, to do justice and judgment; that the LORD may bring upon Abraham that which he hath spoken of him. And the LORD said, Because the cry of Sodom and Gomorrah is great, and because their sin is very grievous; I will go down now, and see whether they have done altogether according to the cry of it, which is come unto me; and if not, I will know (Genesis 18:17-21).

Michael Carasik rightly asks, "How can a God who can see inside the womb not see what was going on in Sodom without going down there?" I had the same question, and Mr. Carasik pointed to a Psalm which contains at least a partial answer.

My substance was not hid from thee, when I was made in secret, and curiously wrought in the lowest parts of the earth. Thine eyes did see my substance, yet being unperfect; and in thy book all my members were written, which in continuance were fashioned, when as yet there was none of them (Psalm 139:15-16).

Later, the Psalmist will plead, "Search me, O God, and know my heart: try me, and know my thoughts: And see if there be any wicked way in me, and lead me in the way everlasting." At first thought, this sounds like he is asking God to read his mind, but the way God read his heart and mind was *indirectly*, by trial.

In other words, know my mind by trying me. The classic illustration of this is Abraham, when he was called on to sacrifice Isaac. The story is familiar, how Abraham took Isaac and went to the place, laid him out for sacrifice and how his hand was stayed at the last moment, God saying, "for now I know that thou fearest God, seeing thou hast not withheld thy son, thine only son from me" (Genesis 22:12).

Are we to conclude from this that God did not know Abraham's mind, that he was not certain of Abraham's devotion until this moment? How can that possibly be? The answer probably lies in the freedom God grants to all men to make their own decisions and run their own lives. Saying that God *can* do something does not necessarily mean that he *will* do it.

I think the answer is that God can read minds but rarely does. He grants man the privacy, the intimacy, if you will, of his own mind, only penetrating when he has a compelling reason to do so. Otherwise we limit God in a different way.

The idea of "omniscience," as held by some people implies that God is unable to *not* know. He cannot close his eyes to the most repugnant acts of man. He was required to observe what went on in every gas chamber in Auschwitz. He had to watch as people's bowels were loosed by death, and he had to watch the bodies burned in the crematorium.

Omniscience does not mean that God has to know. Only that he is able to know if he wishes to know. God does not see everything; not that he cannot, but that he will not. God does not hear everything. God does not see everything. And while he can read your mind, he usually does not care to.

---

i. Bible Review, June, 2002.

ii. Genesis 2:15-17.

iii. Genesis 3:1-7.

iv. Genesis 3:11.

10

God and Time

He has made everything beautiful in its time.
He has also set eternity in the hearts of men;
yet they cannot fathom what God has done
from beginning to end (Ecclesiastes 3:11 NIV).

As I understand my basic science, time can speed up or slow down depending on the speed at which an object travels. That is a little hard to grasp, but they say it has been scientifically demonstrated, so we will take that as a given.

But my proposition is that, fast or slow, time is a one way street. There is no such thing as time travel, nor will there ever be. Time travel is a useful literary device, because it allows an author to develop ideas that cannot otherwise be developed. But in the real world, it will never happen.

The reason for this is simplicity itself. Neither the future nor the past exist. The only reality that *exists* is right now, and it is escaping from us at an alarming rate. I can't go back into the past and see my father again. He is not there any longer. Right now the only way I can go back to my father is to visit the cemetery where he is buried. I had my chance to be with him while he lived, and it is gone. And even though I may get that chance in the future, at the present *time*, it is denied to me.

Time travel is impossible, because there is no other time to travel to. Now I have heard people speak of God existing outside of time, and they draw a mental picture of God sitting on a hill where he can see the entire time line of man. He sees it like a road. We can't see around the next bend, but God sees it all.

But let me pose a problem to consider. As I write this, I am sitting in Tyler, Texas. Can God see me right now, this minute in, say, Mexico City? Of course not, because I am not there, I am here. Have I limited God? Not at all, the original question was an absurdity.

But here comes the stinger: If it is true that God cannot see me right now in Mexico, then can God see me next year? No, not really. I am not there. I am here.

Am I limiting God? Can't God travel in time? Can't God see the future? I suppose he could, but God does not do things merely because he can. So how, then, does God foretell the future? That also is simple. If you had a big enough computer and enough facts, you could easily predict most of the stuff coming down the road. Add to that the simple truth that God can tell us what is going to happen *and then make it happen*, and all becomes clear.

For God to travel into the future, or even for God to see the future, the future must exist. There would have to be a timeline upon which every decision of every man far into the future is known to God. For God to be able to travel to or see the future, the future must exist, right now. Under that assumption, it has already been determined how long you will live and how you will die. Effectively, it means you have no choice about how you will live the rest of your life, it is already known, it is already written.

There have been theologies that assert just that. You have no choice, they say. It has already been written whether you will be saved or lost, whether you will go to hell or heaven, and there is not a thing you can do about it. You are predestined, perhaps to hell.

I was engaged in an Internet discussion about this, and one fellow opined that we have complete free will to make decisions, but God already knows what those decisions will be. Now that is enough to give me a headache. Because for God to know what those decisions will be, they must already be fixed in place. Effectively, you must have already made the decision without knowing it.

Now if you are confused by all this, good for you. You should be.

Let me take you to the Bible and tell you a story which may help clear things up. We will start this story with the assumption that the Bible is true and that God would never deliberately mislead us.

Once upon a time, there was a man named Jonah. He had the unenviable job of being a prophet. Having to prophesy could be downright inconvenient at times, and could lead to very unpleasant outcomes. In this case, God told him to get up and "Arise, go to Nineveh, that great city, and cry out against it; for their wickedness has come up before Me."

For reasons that may not be important right now, Jonah didn't want to do that. So he went down to the harbor, paid his fare, and boarded a ship going in the opposite direction. He wanted to get away from God, foolish man. The story continues with a storm, Jonah being thrown overboard and swallowed by a great fish. Everyone knows that part of the story, so we will pass over it and rejoin Jonah after he is spit out on the beach back where he started.

Now, God speaks to him again: "Arise, go to Nineveh, that great city, and preach to it the message that I tell you" (Jonah 3:2).

Having got the point, Jonah proceeded to Nineveh and began to march through the city preaching the message God told him to give the city. At every step, he cried out: "Yet forty days, and Nineveh shall be overthrown."

This is what God told Jonah to preach. Upon what was the prophetic warning based? Had God traveled into the future and seen what was in store for the great city? Or, was he sitting on the mountain of Time and looked down and saw what was coming on Nineveh?

Assuming that was the case, why tell them? If the future was already written, why not let the poor people alone until the evil day arrives. Telling them would accomplish nothing if the story was already written and fixed – if the future actually existed and God had seen it.

Here is the theory of time that we are examining. The future exists. God can see it and knows what it is going to be, either because he traveled there, or because he has watched the video. But Jonah poses a rather large problem. The prophesied doom never materialized.

That problem is the response of the people of Nineveh. Something very unusual happened. The people believed Jonah. They proclaimed a fast, they put on sackcloth for garments, and everyone was involved from the wealthiest merchant to the common laborer. Even the King of Nineveh got the word and made a decree:

> *Let man and beast be covered with sackcloth, and cry mightily to God; yes, let every one turn from his evil way and from the violence that is in his hands. Who can tell if God will turn and relent, and turn away from His fierce anger, so that we may not perish? (Jonah 3:8-9).*

This was no half hearted response. They didn't even feed their livestock or let the cows graze. It is a classic example of how to repent. The result? "And God saw their works, that they turned from their evil way; and God repented of the evil, that he had said that he would do unto them; and he did it not."

I can't think of an example more devastating to the theory that God sees the future, that the future already exists. If the future were already in place, that future included the repentance of the people of Nineveh and the truth that the city was *not* going to be destroyed. But if that were the true future, then how could God tell Jonah to go and preach that the city would be overthrown?

This creates an insoluble paradox. It is simply not possible. The logic and the scripture are conclusive. Nineveh's future was not there to be seen. It would be determined by the actions of the people and the response of God. Logic and the Bible agree. Neither the future nor the past exist. The past is gone forever, and the future is being built one moment at a time by the decisions and actions of God and man.

That said, there is another angle to be explored. Time is not the same for all men, all the time. How can that be? Let me try to explain.

In the practical world in which you live and have your being, time moves in one direction only. There is nothing in either science or the Bible to suggest otherwise. Taking this a step further, science tells us as a matter of demonstrated fact, that time is not a constant.

Time can speed up and slow down, but it cannot reverse. Science theorizes that as an object approaches the speed of light, time, for that object, slows down. Theoretically, at the speed of light, time stops. Perhaps that is why a particle/wave of light can travel billions of miles in space and not lose any of its energy. No time has passed. How can this be? I haven't a clue.

But there is a scene in the movie, "Close Encounters of the Third Kind," that drops a hint on the savvy viewer. The first space ship ever to arrive on earth from another civilization lands at a remote site and begins to disgorge people who had disappeared decades before, including a squadron of pilots whose planes had disappeared in the Bermuda Triangle.

These aviators came walking off the space ship unharmed and not having aged a day in the decades that had past. There isn't much explanation of this in the movie, but let me explain the idea.

The movie assumes that these pilots and their planes had been taken up by this space ship. The ship, traveling away from the earth at near the speed of light had slowed time for its occupants. Only a few days or perhaps months had passed for the aviators on the ship. Meanwhile, on earth, time had passed at the normal, much faster rate. Everyone the pilots had known had grown old and died, while they hardly aged at all. The aliens then returned the planes to a spot in the desert, preparatory to returning the pilots.

Then comes the close encounter as the space ship arrives, lets off the pilots and the aliens meet the scientists who had figured out what they were doing. It's great fun as science fiction, and *theoretically* possible. But even in the movie, time traveled in only one direction. We did not travel into the past and they did not travel into the future. Our personal times parted and then joined again, having traveled at different speeds in between.

For the aviators, it would have seemed very much like time travel. Their watches kept running. Their hearts kept beating. Time for them seemed unchanged. Then, when they walked off the ship, the world was half a century older. You might call that time travel, but it really isn't. It is time *dilation*.

Time dilation has been demonstrated. Atomic clocks run at a slightly different speed in orbit from what they do here on earth. The reason is that they are traveling faster. So, time is not a constant.

Practically, the difference is very little, but theoretically, it can be much greater.

Now why am I telling you all this? It is to underline the existence of *personal* time. Each of us lives and loves in our own *personal* time. It is a constant for us, no matter what else goes on around us. If one of us were able to travel in space at high speed and return, neither of us would be aware of any change in our personal time. But when we got back to meet each other again, one of us would have aged slightly less than the other.

Then, there is this.

Some years ago, Tennessee Ernie Ford popularized an old spiritual titled, "Just a Closer Walk with Thee." It is surprising how much good, simple theology is contained in folk music and spirituals. One stanza of the song begins:

> When this feeble life is o'er,
> Time for me will be no more.

I had a friend named Ted. He lived in "Ted time," and I live in "Ron time." Ted died a few years ago, and for him, time stopped. For me, it went on. At some time in the future Ted will be raised from the dead to appear before the Lord. In "Ted time," not one second will have passed. In "Ron time," several years will have passed. One minute, Ted was looking up at a nurse in a hospital, and in the next moment of *his* time, he is looking at the face of God. For him, there is no time between these two events.

Standing next to him on the sea of glass, will be all of us who survived him. We will have parted in time, but will come together again in time. Even though for Ted, time stopped, for the rest of us it went on.

And this addresses a misconception in the popular religious culture. Preachers are fond of picturing people up in heaven being able to look down on us in real time. But that is not possible. For them, time has ceased to be and will only start ticking again at the resurrection of the dead. The picture of people who have died going straight to heaven and looking down on us dissolves into absurdity if you think about it logically. After all, people in heaven are supposed to be happy. How could they be looking at the mess we are making of things?

King Solomon, who seems not to take the resurrection into account, speaks of the state of the dead.

> *Anyone who is among the living has hope – even a live dog is better off than a dead lion! For the living know that they will die, but the dead know nothing; they have no further reward, and even the memory of them is forgotten. Their love, their hate and their jealousy have long since vanished; never again will they have a part in anything that happens under the sun (Ecclesiastes 9:4-6 NIV).*

The Greek idea of the immortal soul entered Christian theology early, but it isn't supported in the Bible. Part of the confusion arises from a failure to understand time. Paul addresses it from where he stood. He compared his body to a tabernacle, a tent. The comparison is apt to any tent camper who has seen his tent slowly wear out, poles bent, stakes lost, holes where the field mice ate through.

> *For we know that if our earthly house of this tabernacle were dissolved, we have a building of God, an house not made with hands, eternal in the heavens. For in this we groan, earnestly desiring to be clothed upon with our house which is from heaven: If so be that being clothed we shall not be found naked. For we that are in this tabernacle do groan, being burdened: not for that we would be unclothed, but clothed upon, that mortality might be swallowed up of life (2 Corinthians 5:1-4).*

The aging process takes its toll with arthritic joints, neuropathy in the feet, shortness of breath, sore muscles, and a general slowing down. The body does become an increasing burden as we age. But it is not that Paul doesn't want to *be*. He just wants a better body, for his mortality to be swallowed up in new life. It is easy to identify with that. Paul goes on.

> *Now he that hath wrought us for the selfsame thing is*
> *God, who also hath given unto us the earnest of the*
> *Spirit. Therefore we are always confident, knowing*
> *that, whilst we are at home in the body, we are absent*
> *from the Lord: (For we walk by faith, not by sight.)*

This is easy to understand. In the flesh, a man cannot approach God, cannot actually see God in his glory. For as long as we are flesh, that vision is denied us.

> *We are confident, I say, and willing rather to be*
> *absent from the body, and to be present with the Lord.*
> *Wherefore we labour, that, whether present or absent,*
> *we may be accepted of him. For we must all appear*
> *before the judgment seat of Christ; that every one*
> *may receive the things done in his body, according to*
> *that he hath done, whether it be good or bad.*

The common error with this verse is to assume that when we are dead, we are absent from the body. There is nothing here or elsewhere to suggest that. We are absent from the body at the resurrection of the saints. What happens at death is that time stops. So for all practical purposes, the moment of death is the moment we see God. Paul was ready for that, as he told the Philippian brethren.

> *For to me to live is Christ, and to die is gain. But if I*
> *live in the flesh, this is the fruit of my labour: yet what*
> *I shall choose I wot not. For I am in a strait betwixt*
> *two, having a desire to depart, and to be with Christ;*
> *which is far better: Nevertheless to abide in the flesh*
> *is more needful for you. And having this confidence, I*
> *know that I shall abide and continue with you all for*
> *your furtherance and joy of faith (Philippians*
> *1:21-25).*

Now let me return to my theme of *God and Time*. As it pertains to prophecy, it is clear enough. We have the example of Jonah and Nineveh, but we also have a very specific explanation of how it works in the book of the Prophet Jeremiah.

The Word of the Lord came to Jeremiah and told him to get up and go down to the potter's house. When he got there, the potter was working with a lump of clay on the potter's wheel. While Jeremiah watched, something went wrong and the vessel the potter was making didn't look right. So, he kneaded the clay back into a lump, restarted the wheel and started making something completely different.

About that time, the Lord spoke to Jeremiah, "O house of Israel, cannot I do with you as this potter? saith the LORD. Behold, as the clay is in the potter's hand, so are ye in mine hand, O house of Israel" (see Jeremiah 18:5).

The message is clear. God is sovereign, he can do whatever he wants with you. But then, the Lord outlines the fundamental principle of prophecy:

> *At what instant I shall speak concerning a nation, and concerning a kingdom, to pluck up, and to pull down, and to destroy it; If that nation, against whom I have pronounced, turn from their evil, I will repent of the evil that I thought to do unto them.*

This is the principle at work in Nineveh. There is a lot of information here. God does not destroy nations for no reason at all. Prophecy is to give them a chance to do something different. To repent of their evil ways. If they do, the prophecy will not come to pass, and the small truth that arises from that is that *prophecy is not always about inexorable future events*. Then comes the corollary.

> *And at what instant I shall speak concerning a nation, and concerning a kingdom, to build and to plant it; If it do evil in my sight, that it obey not my voice, then I will repent of the good, wherewith I said I would benefit them.*

So there are two sides to this equation. But in both sides, the outcome of the prophecy is determined by the response of the people to whom it is given. That said, there is a danger here exemplified by the response of the people to Jeremiah's prophecy. They said, "*There is no hope*: but we will walk after our own devices, and we will every one do the imagination of his evil heart."

There is no hope, they say, so why bother repenting. In a way, this is what people say who insist that the future already exists and the prophet has seen it. What's the point in even trying, they say, God has already made up his mind about me.

Not so. What the prophet has seen is what will happen if there is no change. And that is what Jonah's message was. There is a bridge out ahead, and you need to hit the brakes.

When you read the prophets, you can conclude that much of what they say may be a prediction based on human behavior with the rest involving divine intervention. *It will happen*, but not because God already saw it.

The folly of trying to set dates for the events in prophecy is that things change. For example, Ninevah finally was overthrown. Jonah turned out to be right after all, *except for the forty days*. Jesus' disciples asked a comparable question. When he warned that the day would come when the Temple would be destroyed, the disciples asked the obvious questions: When will this happen, and how will we know it is near?

Jesus gave them a litany of end time events, including a time called the Great Tribulation. The disciples' question hung in the air: When will it happen? Jesus' answer is proverbial:

> *Now learn a parable of the fig tree; When his branch is yet tender, and putteth forth leaves, ye know that summer is nigh: So likewise ye, when ye shall see all these things, know that it is near, even at the doors. Verily I say unto you, This generation shall not pass, till all these things be fulfilled. Heaven and earth shall pass away, but my words shall not pass away. But of that day and hour knoweth no man, no, not the angels of heaven, but my Father only (Matthew 24:32-36).*

There is nothing arcane or hidden here. You will see the harbingers of the last day, but the timing is subject to change. People have taken Jesus to mean that God has a calendar, and he has marked the day of Jesus' return, but kept it secret, even from the angels. What God has marked down is the predictable direction of human events, but he has not taken away from man the possibility of repentance. Sooner or later, he will have to intervene, but we can't know when that will be for the simple reason that it may not be set in concrete.

"And unless those days were shortened," Jesus went on to say, "no flesh would be saved; but for the elect's sake those days will be shortened." In other words, if God lets things run their normal course, we will end up killing everyone. The return of Christ is a rescue operation, to save us from ourselves. But the date is unknown, because we must have room to repent.

I get the feeling that some preachers will be like Jonah. They will be upset if people repent and God relents. Maybe God can let them have their holocaust and save the rest of us.

So, we conclude God is in charge of time. We know, and we know that we know, that the past no longer exists. People who lived a hundred years ago aren't sitting back there waiting on us to come back to visit. They are dead. We can also conclude that the future doesn't exist for exactly the same reason the past doesn't exist. It may make good fiction, but fiction is not life. Time travel would not be merely traveling in time, it would be traveling to another world, a world that does not exist.

The future does not exist. It is being created, one moment at a time by decisions we make and the decisions God makes. That being true, then, the decisions you make become very important. Your future is not already written. You are writing it right now. There is no fate, waiting for you inexorably.

The people Jeremiah spoke to were wrong when they said, "There is no hope." After David's adulterous fling with Bathsheba, after her husband was killed by David's machinations, God told him through Nathan the prophet that the child would die. That was a prophecy. It did come to pass. But David never said, "There is no hope." When the child finally died, he had this to say:

> *While the child was yet alive, I fasted and wept: for I said, Who can tell whether GOD will be gracious to me, that the child may live? But now he is dead,*

83

> *wherefore should I fast? can I bring him back again?*
> *I shall go to him, but he shall not return to me (2*
> *Samuel 12:22).*

Be careful about the history you are writing today. Tomorrow is in *your* hands.

11

God and Man

Up from the bed of the river God scooped the clay;
And by the bank of the river He kneeled Him down;
And there the great God Almighty
Who lit the sun and fixed it in the sky,
Who flung the stars to the most far corner of the night,
Who rounded the earth in the middle of His hand;
This Great God, Like a mammy bending over her baby,
Kneeled down in the dust Toiling over a lump of clay
Till He shaped it in His own image;
Then into it He blew the breath of life,
And man became a living soul. ⁱ

Is anything too hard for God? I wouldn't think so. But it seems there are certain limitations he has placed on himself, and these are things that concern man. When he made man, God created plenty of limitations. It is, therefore, no simple thing to reveal himself to man.

For one thing, if God in all his power gets too close to a man, after moment of sizzling, there is no more man. For another, there are some ideas, easily held by God, that man is utterly unable to grasp. Perhaps because there are not enough brain cells. Perhaps because these ideas are so far outside any experience of man that there is no frame of reference.

God obviously knew what he was doing when he made man, and he knew where he was going with the project. Right from the beginning, he had to take himself down somewhat in order to interact with Adam, and later with Abraham. With Adam and Eve, God closed his eyes and gave them some privacy. With Abraham, he came as a man and ate with him before discussing the fate of Sodom. In Moses' case, he came in the midst of the burning bush. Then, at Mount Sinai, everyone heard his voice and never wanted to hear it again. On another occasion, he allowed the governing elders of Israel see him.

> *Then went up Moses, and Aaron, Nadab, and Abihu, and seventy of the elders of Israel: And they saw the God of Israel: and there was under his feet as it were a paved work of a sapphire stone, and as it were the body of heaven in his clearness. And upon the nobles of the children of Israel he laid not his hand: also they saw God, and did eat and drink (Exodus 24:9-11).*

On still another occasion, Moses was allowed to see his back only, because no one could look upon God's face and live – there was just too much power there. [ii] So you can see what I mean when I say that it is no simple matter for God to reveal himself. Even in these events, the person of God is only seen in a limited way.

Men knew God from his mighty works. They knew God from his law. But what was he really like? How can we really know him? How could God get really close to man, and how could he make it possible for man to get *really* close to him?

The events that answer this question are well enough known. God became flesh and walked among us. Men were able to see him, hear him, even to touch him and be touched by him. The story of the nativity of Jesus has been repeated over and over again, and may even suffer a bit from too much familiarity. You may even be able to recite what the angel Gabriel said to Mary:

> *Fear not, Mary: for thou hast found favour with God. And, behold, thou shalt conceive in thy womb, and*

bring forth a son, and shalt call his name JESUS. He shall be great, and shall be called the Son of the Highest: and the Lord God shall give unto him the throne of his father David: And he shall reign over the house of Jacob for ever; and of his kingdom there shall be no end (Luke 1:30-33).

Mary was troubled, but had the presence of mind to ask how this was possible, seeing she had not slept with a man. Gabriel replied, *"The Holy Spirit will come upon you, and the power of the Highest will overshadow you; therefore, also, that Holy One who is to be born will be called the Son of God" (Luke 1:35 NKJV).*

We are accustomed to the expression, "Son of God," but the idea of a "Son of the Highest" is less familiar. The word is *hupistos*, which is masculine singular, and it points squarely toward the Father. Jesus was later identified by a demoniac who cried aloud, *"What have I to do with thee, Jesus, thou Son of the most high God? I adjure thee by God, that thou torment me not" (Mark 5:7).*

When the time came for Jesus to be born, the process was all very deliberate. To all outward appearances, this was an ordinary child, a child of lowly birth. The birth was not announced to royalty or to the priestly establishment in Jerusalem. The first public acknowledgment of this birth was to a handful of sheep herders near Bethlehem. It is important to know that the shepherds knew what it meant when the angel said, "unto you is born this day in the city of David a Saviour, which is Christ the Lord" (Luke 2:11).

The angel went on to tell them that there would be something significant about where they would find this child, their Lord. They would find him in a stable, in a feeding trough. What this means is that the circumstances of his birth were lowly. He came, not like a king would come, but as one of the poorest of us. At the same time, he was the "Son of the Highest." What did that mean?

Whatever the appearances, this was no ordinary child, and Jesus was no ordinary man. Late in his ministry, the Jews were pressing him to tell them plainly whether he was the Messiah or not. Jesus' answer was electrifying to the Jews, so much so that they actually picked up stones to kill him. What did he say that incensed them so?

> *I told you, and ye believed not: the works that I do in
> my Father's name, they bear witness of me. But ye
> believe not, because ye are not of my sheep, as I said
> unto you. My sheep hear my voice, and I know them,
> and they follow me: And I give unto them eternal life;
> and they shall never perish, neither shall any man
> pluck them out of my hand. My Father, which gave
> them me, is greater than all; and no man is able to
> pluck them out of my Father's hand. I and my Father
> are one (John 10:24-30).*

The Jews were about to stone Jesus because, in their words,
"that you, being a man, make yourself God." Any ordinary man at
the time would have torn his garments and denied that he made
any such claim. Jesus did not deny it. Instead, he said:

> *Is it not written in your law, I said, Ye are gods? If he
> called them gods, unto whom the word of God came,
> and the scripture cannot be broken; Say ye of him,
> whom the Father hath sanctified, and sent into the
> world, Thou blasphemest; because I said, I am the
> Son of God? If I do not the works of my Father,
> believe me not. But if I do, though ye believe not me,
> believe the works: that ye may know, and believe, that
> the Father is in me, and I in him (John 10:34-39).*

The Jews understood clearly that Jesus, in claiming to be the
Son of God, was claiming to *be* God. What we are seeing here is the
ultimate move by God to reveal himself to man.

Perhaps the most striking example of the way Jesus' disciples
came to understand this is found in the opening statements of the
book of Hebrews. The author (assumed by many to be Paul) had this
to say:

> *God, who at sundry times and in divers manners
> spake in time past unto the fathers by the prophets,
> Hath in these last days spoken unto us by his Son,
> whom he hath appointed heir of all things, by whom*

also he made the worlds; Who being the brightness of
his glory, and the express image of his person, and
upholding all things by the word of his power, when
he had by himself purged our sins, sat down on the
right hand of the Majesty on high (Hebrews 1:1-8).

He goes on to question the relationship of the Son to the angels. God said to none of the angels, "You are my Son, this day have I begotten you."

In this passage, there is an important grammatical structure that is easy to miss. First, establish the antecedent of the pronouns: "For unto which of the angels said *he* at any time." "He" is the Father. And it is the Father speaking through a series of parallel phrases.

- Thou art my Son, this day have I begotten thee.
- I will be to him a Father, and he shall be to me a Son.
- When he bringeth in the firstbegotten into the world, he saith, "And let all the angels of God worship him."
- But unto the Son he saith, Thy throne, O God, is for ever and ever: a sceptre of righteousness is the sceptre of thy kingdom.
- And [it is the Father continuing to speak], Thou, Lord, in the beginning hast laid the foundation of the earth; and the heavens are the works of thine hands:"

There is no misunderstanding this passage. The Father is calling the Son "God." Not only that, but he attributes to him the laying of the foundations of the earth. John, in his Gospel, addresses this issue in the very first verse.

In the beginning was the Word, and the Word was
with God, and the Word was God. The same was in
the beginning with God. All things were made by him;
and without him was not any thing made that was
made" (John 1:1-3).

We might misunderstand this if it were not for what follows in verses 10-14.

He was in the world, and the world was made by him,
and the world knew him not. He came unto his own,
and his own received him not. . . And the Word was
made flesh, and dwelt among us, (and we beheld his
glory, the glory as of the only begotten of the Father,)
full of grace and truth.

So Jesus was God in the flesh. For some people, this is logically impossible. God can't become flesh. God can't die. But He not only could, he did. Why limit God? Jesus was completely human, only divested of his glory and power so man could touch him, and so he could die. But the divestiture did not change who he was: He was God in the flesh.

The western mind, which explains everything and understands nothing, can't accept the paradox of Jesus being all human and all God at the same time. The eastern mind, to whom John was writing, understands that there are some realities that defy rational explanation.

But the author of Hebrews is not finished telling us about the Son. Chapter two continues with a warning that we should give all the more earnest attention to the things we have heard lest they get away from us. "How shall we escape," he asks, "if we neglect so great salvation?"

It is a shame that Christians have become so locked up in their jargon that they have lost the original sense of these words. Salvation, in its most basic sense means deliverance, which in turn means liberation. A savior, then, is a liberator. Consider what that meant to the shepherds who heard the angel say, "Unto you is born this day in the city of David, a liberator, who is Christ the Lord." A nation and people occupied by their Roman overlords yearned for liberty. And for them, salvation would always be compared to their liberation from Egypt.

An old Christian hymn cries, "I am saved." That's not far from Martin Luther King's: "Free at last, thank God almighty, free at last."

---

i. "The Creation," James Weldon Johnson.

ii. See Exodus 33:18-23.

12

The Great Misunderstanding

*Do not think that I have come to abolish the Law or the
Prophets; I have not come to abolish them but to fulfill
them. I tell you the truth, until heaven and earth
disappear, not the smallest letter, not the least stroke of
a pen, will by any means disappear from the Law until
everything is come to pass [i] (Matthew 5:17-18).*

Jesus spoke to this vexing question quite early and in one of
his most definitive sermons. The statement cited above is clear and
unambiguous, and yet the question of the law for Christians has been
a headache for generations.

But when you think carefully about what Jesus said, it is not
merely the law, but also the prophets. He is speaking to the authority
of what we today would call "The Old Testament." It is worth asking
why he felt it necessary to issue this clarification. Obviously, he was
concerned that people would think something erroneous and he
wanted to head that off right from the start.

The Old Testament, would not be abolished, said Jesus. And
for us, that means we have to take the Bible as a whole, not dividing
it up into parts, some of which we heed and some of which we ignore.
What that means is that we take both the Bible and the Law of God as
a whole. The next thing it means is that there are Old Testament laws
that Christians should still obey.

When I first came to understand this, it opened a major door of understanding. But it was, in a way, like picking a lock and getting inside only to find a maze of corridors. There were laws that anyone could plainly see they should keep (Thou shalt not steal). And there were laws that were, to put it bluntly, repugnant to the modern mind (slavery). There were even laws that made no sense at all.

The solution to this problem varies depending on the person addressing the problem:

1. The entire Old Testament was done away in Christ.
2. The Ten Commandments were abolished in the New Testament, and nine of them were reinstated.
3. The ritual law was done away, but the moral law retained.
4. The law of Moses was abolished, the Law of God retained.
5. The law was abolished with the Old Covenant and we live under the New Covenant.
6. We are not under the law but under grace.

And I am sure there are any number of variations on the theme. Protagonists argue these ideas, establishing and buttressing them with an array of proof texts. The problem is, that the other side is also established and buttressed with an array of proof texts. The buttresses have only grown higher over the years as both sides build their defenses against attacks from the other side.

The positions are hardened beyond breaching, but the entire structure of the debate is built on a simple misunderstanding. Both sides built their positions on the same premise, and that premise was wrong. They seem to have missed what Jesus was driving at when he said, "until heaven and earth disappear, not the smallest letter, not the least stroke of a pen, will by any means disappear from the Law." He added, "until everything is come to pass," which merely reinforces the permanence of the law.

In my own journey to understanding, I finally concluded that most of the arguments about the law, from both sides of the issue, are rendered pointless right here in this short statement. You *cannot* abolish one part of the law and keep another. Why? Because heaven and earth have not passed away. You can't toss out "the law of Moses" and keep "the Law of God." You can't arbitrarily toss out nine of the Ten Commandments.

Now I know all too well what enormous problems I have raised here. Because once you embark on a study of divine law, huge problems present themselves. But only if you are still laboring under the Great Misunderstanding, which is: The concept that the law was ever, at any time, an instrument of salvation, that if you broke any jot or tittle of the law, you lost salvation, that God would come down on you with the death penalty.

There are two important instances that illustrate that was not the case. One is Abraham's lie.[ii] He told Pharoah, "Sarah is my sister," which was not true. It had temporal consequences, but no lasting penalty and no rift in Abraham's relationship with God. Another is David eating the showbread which, in Jesus' words, [iii] was not lawful for him to eat. It had temporal consequences in that it got some people killed, but again, no lasting penalty, and even Jesus seems to dismiss it.

So what is the deal? Why do some people "Get away with it" and others don't? If you want to understand the purpose of the Law of God, get yourself a cup of coffee, a Bible, and a comfortable chair. Then read slowly and thoughtfully through the 119th Psalm. Here is a man who really understood and appreciated the purpose of the law.

And the sum total of the Great Misunderstanding is summarized in one verse of this great Psalm: "Your word is a lamp to my feet and a light for my path" (Psalm 119:105). The purpose of the law is not to control, but to teach. The law is a guide to life, a definer of sin. Sin is what hurts, destroys and ruins lives. The Law of God is not shackles and chains. It is *light*. It is not a yoke of bondage, it is a *lamp*.

Jesus was at some pains to point out that the Pharisees didn't understand the law. One of his great indictments of the sect had to do with the way they bound the law on other men when they wouldn't follow their own rules:

> *The scribes and the Pharisees sit in Moses' seat: All therefore whatsoever they bid you observe, that observe and do; but do not ye after their works: for they say, and do not. For they bind heavy burdens and grievous to be borne, and lay them on men's shoulders; but they themselves will not move them*

with one of their fingers (Matthew 23:2-4).

The scribes and Pharisees held judicial authority for the religious community, an authority they were abusing. Contrast this with Jesus' approach:

> *Come unto me, all ye that labour and are heavy laden, and I will give you rest. Take my yoke upon you, and learn of me; for I am meek and lowly in heart: and ye shall find rest unto your souls. For my yoke is easy, and my burden is light (Matthew 11:28-30).*

Now let me show you an example out of the law to demonstrate what I mean. Moses' law included some culture specific items that would seem to make no sense in the modern world. One, for example required the Israelites to place a blue ribbon on the borders of their garments. The law had a specific purpose:

> *Speak unto the children of Israel, and bid them that they make them fringes in the borders of their garments throughout their generations, and that they put upon the fringe of the borders a ribband of blue: And it shall be unto you for a fringe, that ye may look upon it, and remember all the commandments of the LORD, and do them; and that ye seek not after your own heart and your own eyes, after which ye use to go a whoring (Numbers 15:38-39).*

The Hebrew for "fringe" means "a floral or wing-like projection." They were worn to be seen. There are people to this day who wear a blue ribbon somewhere on their garment because of this law. Now I don't want to hurt your feelings or embarrass anyone, but if you are wearing a blue tassel on your underwear, you are being a little silly for two reasons. One, no one can see it, so it is pointless. Two, it doesn't mean anything in our society anyhow. Try it. Wear a little ribbon of blue on your lapel and see if anyone says, "Oh, I see that you are a commandment keeper." What does society have to do with it? More than you might think.

The law also said, "*A woman must not wear men's clothing, nor a man wear women's clothing, for the Lord your God detests anyone who does this" (Deuteronomy 22:5)*. I once heard a discussion on this where a gentleman asked, quite aptly, "Where in the law does it say that the fabric must go around each leg for a man, but encompass both legs for woman?" He knew how silly he sounded, but that was his point. It was silly. The law does not determine what clothing is appropriate for a woman or a man. Culture does that. The point of the law is that gender identity is important.

Here is what you need to know about the ribbon of blue. The blue ribbon was an insignia, and anyone who has ever been in the military knows what an insignia is. It can be a designation of rank, your unit, and even of the job you hold in that unit. Three chevrons on the sleeve of an infantryman, along with a shoulder patch displaying a large red number 1, means that the man is a sergeant in the first infantry division.

There was an occasion when David, hiding from Saul in a cave, found Saul coming into that cave to relieve himself (1 Samuel 24:1 ff.). While he could have killed Saul, he didn't. Instead, he cut off the hem of Saul's robe – very likely, his insignia. It was a significant act, for the kingdom now belonged to David anyhow.

We have a curious civilian insignia that has developed in our society in recent years. It is the yellow ribbon. It did not originate with the Tony Orlando song. It goes at least as far back as the American Cavalry during the Indian wars. You may know the tune to the song, "She wore a yellow ribbon." Some think the custom had to do with yellow stripe on the leg of a cavalryman.

In recent years, the idea has spread to where we know that when we see a ribbon worn in particular way, looped over and forming a floral or winglike projection, we know it means something. It may mean that the bearer supports our troops – or has a loved one in harm's way, perhaps a lover in the US *Armored* Cavalry. We recognize pink ribbons that support research for breast cancer, and I suppose the green ribbon I saw had something to do with the environment.

It is possible if God were handing down this law today, he would tell us to wear a blue ribbon in our lapel or over our heart for the same reason he told Israel to wear the blue *tsitsit*. As an insignia. I think it is important to realize that this was not merely a personal reminder. I have the Holy Spirit to remind me of God's law *personally*. For Israel, I think it was to remind them that they were a *society where the Law of God is the organizing principle.*

If I wore the ribbon today, I would not be wearing the ribbon for me. I would be wearing it for you. But if we wore one today, it would be meaningless, almost dishonest, because we are *not* a society where the Law of God is the guiding light.

On the other hand, it could be useful for evangelism. Someone might ask, "What does your blue ribbon mean?" You could answer, "It means that the Law of God is a lamp to my feet and a light to my path. That the Law of God as taught by Jesus Christ, is the guiding principle of my life."

And this illustration is helpful in clearing up the Great Misunderstanding. We do not slavishly follow the letter of the law. It was Paul who clarified this for us.

> *For when we were in the flesh, the motions of sins, which were by the law, did work in our members to bring forth fruit unto death. But now we are delivered from the law, that being dead wherein we were held; that we should serve in newness of spirit, and not in the oldness of the letter. What shall we say then? is the law sin? God forbid. Nay, I had not known sin, but by the law: for I had not known lust, except the law had said, Thou shalt not covet" (Romans 7:5-7).*

We serve in the spirit and intent of the law. That means we look for the meaning of the law, not the technical letter of the law.

> *Not that we are sufficient of ourselves to think any thing as of ourselves; but our sufficiency is of God; Who also hath made us able ministers of the new testament; not of the letter, but of the spirit: for the letter killeth, but the spirit giveth life" (2 Corinthians 3:5-6).*

96

Someone once said to me: "But that means we get to decide what laws we will keep and what laws we will not keep." Not really. It means we get to decide *how* we will use the law, not whether. We do not use the law as an instrument of salvation, but as a guide to life's decisions, as the definer of sin and righteousness.

So most of the arguments about which laws are "binding" completely miss the point. The problem arose in the New Testament because of *Jewish* law that rose up to tell you how to keep *God's* law. And we misunderstand Paul, because we fail to realize that he is often addressing, not God's law, but Jewish law. As to the Law of God, he said, *"Do we then make void the law through faith? God forbid: yea, we establish the law" (Romans 3:31).*

Returning now to the statement of Jesus cited at the beginning; he is about to embark on *a major revision in the explanation of the law* and he does not want to be misunderstood.

> *Do not think that I have come to abolish the Law or the Prophets; I have not come to abolish them but to fulfill them. I tell you the truth, until heaven and earth disappear, not the smallest letter, not the least stroke of a pen, will by any means disappear from the Law until everything is accomplished. Anyone who breaks one of the least of these commandments and teaches others to do the same will be called least in the kingdom of heaven, but whoever practices and teaches these commands will be called great in the kingdom of heaven (Matthew 5:17 ff.).*

The great puzzle for many people is how it is possible for someone who breaks one of the commandments to even be in the kingdom of heaven, much less be one of the least there. There are some tortured explanations of this verse, but let's consider as a possibility the simplest explanation: The law is not an instrument of salvation.

There will be people who have trusted in Christ for their salvation who, through confusion or ignorance break the commandments and teach others to break them. God, in his mercy may still save. Which of us will tell him he cannot?

This has been the path I followed in clearing up, for me, the Great Misunderstanding. I realize that, for some, it just won't satisfy. But take your time. Someday, it may.

---

i. Greek, *ginomai*. The KJV rendering, "fulfilled" is inconsistent. Elsewhere, this verb is almost universally rendered "come to pass."

ii. See Genesis 12.

iii. Matthew 12:4.

13

The God Who Was One of Us

*"In the beginning was the Word,
and the Word was with God,
and the Word was God."*

Verse one of the Gospel of John is one of the most loaded sentences in the entire Bible. There aren't many places in the Bible where the various translators agree, but this is one of them. Word for word, from the *King James Version* through the most popular modern translations, they present this formulation of the Word. At first blush, it is an enigma. The Word was with God and was God. It is like being beside himself.

Without this opening statement, though, we might easily go astray. John could just as easily have stopped with, "The Word was with God," and we might have seen the Word in one way. Or he could have simply said, "The Word was God," and we would come away thinking that "The Word" was just another of the many names of God.

But in saying the Word was with God and was God, John forces us to consider how that can be. The simplest explanation is usually the best, and leads naturally to the conclusion that "God" is a *kind* of being of which there are at least two. But for a Jew, that was an utter impossibility. For them, the oneness of God was a primary article of faith.[i] How this conundrum is resolved, and where it leads, is one of the great stories of the New Testament.

The story is familiar from endless repetition. An angel of God appeared to a woman named Mary with an announcement so strange that Mary at first couldn't even imagine it.

> *And the angel said unto her, Fear not, Mary: for thou hast found favour with God. And, behold, thou shalt conceive in thy womb, and bring forth a son, and shalt call his name JESUS. He shall be great, and shall be called the Son of the Highest: and the Lord God shall give unto him the throne of his father David: And he shall reign over the house of Jacob for ever; and of his kingdom there shall be no end"* (Luke 1:30-33).

This statement was pregnant with messianic symbols. His name was to be "Yah Saves," he was the Son of the Highest, he would have the throne of David, and his kingdom would have no end. None of this was lost on Mary, but in her question she reveals her expectations of the Messiah, *"How shall this be, seeing I know not a man?"* In Jewish thought of the time, the Messiah would be a man begotten by a son of David. He would be a man anointed of God to save his people. But Mary had never lain with a man. She was a virgin.

The angel had a ready reply: *"The Holy Ghost shall come upon thee, and the power of the Highest shall overshadow thee: therefore also that holy thing which shall be born of thee shall be called the Son of God."*

A myriad of questions can flow from this, but we need to stay on point and follow this through. The Son of God was to be born of a woman. But what was he to be, really? Would he be God, would he be man? The Jews would take Jesus' claim to be the Son of God quite literally. To them, that was a claim of divinity. But then, if he was truly God, was he truly man?

Perhaps the best way to resolve this is to follow on from the events just described in Luke. A Roman decree forced the birth of Jesus to the important town of Bethlehem, the city of David. This was a crucial footnote on Jesus' genealogy.

"But you, Bethlehem Ephrathah, though you are small among the clans of Judah, out of you will come for me one who will be ruler over Israel, whose origins are from of old, from ancient times." [ii]

Born in Bethlehem, the "house of bread" in Hebrew, was the one who would be the bread of life. He was born there, where he was supposed to be born, and because of the decree of the Romans, he was born at a time when Bethlehem was so crowded there was no room in any house for his mother, "great with child," to lie down. Joseph and Mary ended up bedding down in a stable.

Even in the familiar expression, "great with child," there is a revelation of the humanity of the one to be born. He would not step into this world from another world, fully grown. And make no mistake about it, this was possible. God had entered this world just that way on occasion. [iii] It rather boggles the mind to think of Jesus as a fetus, unborn, his bulk causing his mother to walk as you have seen many pregnant women walk, with hand to her back for support. If there had been an ultrasound taken of the baby Mary was carrying, it would have looked like any other male child, perhaps even sucking his thumb – the medical technician would have told Mary, "Honey, you are going to have a boy."

"And so it was, that, while they were there, the days were accomplished that she should be delivered. And she brought forth her firstborn son, and wrapped him in swaddling clothes, and laid him in a manger; because there was no room for them in the inn" (Luke 2:6-7). We are spared the scene of labor, the crowning of the child, the cutting of the cord. Just this simple statement of humble birth. How could one be born in any lower circumstances than to be laid in straw in the feeding trough of the animals? One wonders what the cattle thought of all these goings on in their stable, and how Mary and Joseph felt, enjoying all the smells and sounds of that place.

Everything about this is important for *our* sakes. For this Jesus, Son of God, was also Son of Man, and he was born just as the lowliest of us are born. Exactly like every human baby ever born, he was completely vulnerable and dependent on his mother for survival. As Mary took him to her breast for the first time, it must have been with a sense of great wonder.

Now considering the greatness of this child, how should the announcement be made? Shall we tell the governor and the High Priest in Jerusalem that the Messiah is born? Hardly, and this also is significant. This child was not wrapped in silk and his birth was not announced to the great. The first announcement of the birth of Jesus was made by angels who doubtless felt that they had to tell someone or burst, and the word was given to a handful of sheep herders camped out overnight nearby. The angel who came to tell the shepherds, nearly scared them to death because he appeared suddenly with a burst of great light.

> *And the angel said unto them, Fear not: for, behold, I bring you good tidings of great joy, which shall be to all people. For unto you is born this day in the city of David a Saviour, which is Christ the Lord. And this shall be a sign unto you; Ye shall find the babe wrapped in swaddling clothes, lying in a manger.*

Before the shepherds could close their mouths, a huge gathering of heavenly beings appeared, shouting and singing, *"Glory to God in the highest, and on earth peace, good will toward men."* This verse provides a great musical moment in Handel's "Messiah," but that can't touch what these shepherds heard and saw. We don't have choirs that big.

But stepping back for a moment from the joy of the birth, it is worth noting that the shepherds recognized the significance of this announcement. The angel did not call the town, "Bethlehem." He called it "The city of David." By itself, this was a pointer to the Messiah, but why was it a sign that Jesus was lying in a manger? This wasn't merely so they would know which baby was the one. "This shall be *significant* to you," as it should indeed be significant to us.

So the shepherds made their way to the stable, and when they got there, they found Mary, Joseph, and a baby, lying in a manger. And that was the story they told abroad after that night.

So, Jesus was a baby, entirely dependent on his mother, and all you mothers know precisely what this means. Jesus was helpless and totally vulnerable. Joseph and Mary had to flee to Egypt to prevent that evil, despicable snake, Herod from killing the child along with all the babies around Bethlehem. He could have been destroyed as a child.

Jesus was completely at risk in the world. He was not superman. His nature and the reason for it is described plainly in the Book of Hebrews:

> *Forasmuch then as the children are partakers of flesh and blood, he also himself likewise took part of the same; that through death he might destroy him that had the power of death, that is, the devil; And deliver them who through fear of death were all their lifetime subject to bondage. For verily he took not on him the nature of angels; but he took on him the seed of Abraham. Wherefore in all things it behoved him to be made like unto his brethren, that he might be a merciful and faithful high priest in things pertaining to God, to make reconciliation for the sins of the people. For in that he himself hath suffered being tempted, he is able to succour them that are tempted"* (Hebrews 2:14-18).

Jesus could have failed. He was flesh. This is the reason an angel was sent to him in Gethsemane, to see to it that he didn't fail. You have probably been to the circus and have seen a man walking on a high wire. Think about it. Is it the same when he walks that wire with a net, as it is when he walks it without a net? Jesus' high wire walk was done without a net.

> *Seeing then that we have a great high priest, that is passed into the heavens, Jesus the Son of God, let us hold fast our profession. For we have not an high priest which cannot be touched with the feeling of our infirmities; but was in all points tempted like as we are, yet without sin. Let us therefore come boldly unto the throne of grace, that we may obtain mercy, and find grace to help in time of need (Hebrews 4:14-16).*

Whatever the path you walk, Jesus walked it before you.

Whatever pain you suffer in life, Jesus suffered it before you. And if you want him to, he will walk your path with you. And he will suffer with you.

> *Beloved, believe not every spirit, but try the spirits whether they are of God: because many false prophets are gone out into the world. Hereby know ye the Spirit of God: Every spirit that confesseth that Jesus Christ is come in the flesh is of God: And every spirit that confesseth not that Jesus Christ is come in the flesh is not of God: and this is that spirit of antichrist, whereof ye have heard that it should come; and even now already is it in the world (1 John 4:1-3).*

---

i. "Hear, O Israel! The LORD is our God, the LORD is one!" (Deuteronomy 6:4 NASB)

ii. Micah 5:2 NIV; Bethlehem in Hebrew is the "House of Bread" and Ephrathah means, "Fruitful."

iii. See Genesis 18.

14

The Healer

Bless the LORD, O my soul: and all that is within me, bless his holy name. Bless the LORD, O my soul, and forget not all his benefits: Who forgiveth all thine iniquities; who healeth all thy diseases (Psalm 103:1-3).

Does God still heal the sick? I think most people believe that he does. Most people believe in prayer and they believe in miracles, they just don't think they happen very often. And they believe in healing "merely" as an answer to prayer or a miracle. There is no distinct *meaning* connected to healing.

I think it's possible, though, that many people are troubled by an alternate question. Since God certainly can heal, why does he do it so rarely? Because for every wonderful healing in answer to prayer, there are many that go unanswered and many people we loved and prayed for have died. And there seems to be no way to account for the arbitrary way in which these healings take place – or don't.

Oh, I know there are some that are obvious. For one thing, everyone has to die eventually. We have the record in the Bible that Elisha fell sick of the sickness whereof he died, and there was never a more powerful prophet. But what is it with divine healing that we don't understand?

One of the most striking things about this question is that we could have asked the very same question of Jesus when he was engaged in his ministry. Recognizing his power, it is not surprising that he healed people. It is surprising that he didn't heal everyone all the time. If you have the power and you have the compassion, why not heal? I don't think I could bring myself to visit a veterans' hospital and heal one or two people. I would want to empty the place.

Why didn't Jesus do the same?

You may know the story. Jesus came into his own country, taught in their synagogues and was largely dismissed, leading to Jesus' familiar saying "A prophet is not without honour, save in his own country, and in his own house." Matthew goes on to tell us, "He did not many mighty works there because of their unbelief" (Matthew 13:58).

Was this a choice on Jesus' part? Could he have done miracles, but decided not to because of their unbelief? Apparently not. Outlining this same event, Mark notes, "And he could there do no mighty work, save that he laid his hands upon a few sick folk, and healed them" (Mark 6:5).

The Greek construction of this remark implies that it *was not possible* for him to do any mighty work. Literally, the scripture says he was powerless, which is a very strange thing to say about Jesus.

It seems likely that God has an override switch. That is to say, he can do a miracle if he chooses no matter what the conditions. But in the normal course of events, it is not good for him to do a healing in the face of *settled unbelief.* Unbelief and doubt are not the same thing.

On another occasion, Jesus came upon his disciples surrounded by a crowd and being questioned by some scribes. A man came and explained to Jesus: "*Master, I have brought unto thee my son, which hath a dumb spirit; And wheresoever he taketh him, he teareth him: and he foameth, and gnasheth with his teeth, and pineth away: and I spake to thy disciples that they should cast him out; and they could not*" (Mark 9:17-18)

Now this young man was a pitiful case. The disciples had been unable to deal with him, and Jesus probably included them in what he called a "faithless generation."

"If thou canst do any thing," the man pleaded, "have compassion on us, and help us." What happened next is instructive:

*Jesus said unto him, If thou canst believe, all things
are possible to him that believeth. And straightway
the father of the child cried out, and said with tears,
Lord, I believe; help thou mine unbelief.*

We understand this fellow well enough. He believed, he just
wasn't so sure of his belief. I think there is a distinction between the
settled unbelief, which makes miracles impossible, and the doubts
which beset us all from time to time. Unbelief, as the Bible uses the
term, is not the same thing as uncertainty. It is disbelief.

If I am not certain that God will heal me when I pray, that
does not make me an unbeliever, nor does it mean that I lack faith. It
means that I am not certain of God's plan and intent. But *if I am
placing my trust in him no matter what the outcome, that is faith.*

The role of faith is obviously very important. On another
occasion, Jesus had retreated to the coast around Tyre, seeking a little
peace and quiet. But, as Mark puts it, he could not be hid. A woman
came to him and fell at his feet. She pleaded with Jesus to cast a devil
out of her daughter. This is a truly remarkable incident, because Jesus
initially *refused*. "Let the children first be filled:" he said, "for it is not
meet to take the children's bread, and to cast it unto the dogs."

This seems totally out of character. Not only does he refuse,
he does so in terms that seem calculated to be offensive. But the
woman refused to be offended.

*And she answered and said unto him, Yes, Lord: yet
the dogs under the table eat of the children's crumbs.
And he said unto her, For this saying go thy way; the
devil is gone out of thy daughter. And when she was
come to her house, she found the devil gone out, and
her daughter laid upon the bed (Mark 7:28-30).*

In this case, it is a decision Jesus can make. He was not sent
to Gentiles, but he plainly had the power and authority to override
that principle. And he did so in the face of faith, belief, *and
persistence,* all of which seem to be important for healing.

We all know these things. But what is it about healing that is
different from other miracles? Jesus turned water into wine. He

walked on the water. I hadn't thought about it until someone pointed it out to me years ago. Healing is different in that it involves *the restoration of something that has gone wrong.*

God did not create man to be sick. It is not God's way to create a blind man. He did not create man crippled. He created man perfect, but something has gone terribly wrong.

Now I have noted that Jesus did not always heal. Let me take the question a step further. Since he didn't have to heal to accomplish his mission, why did Jesus heal at all? Some people think it is a kind of advertising. Jesus healed a man to gather a crowd so he could preach. I think that cheapens what Jesus was doing.

Why, then, did Jesus heal? Consider another example. Luke tells us that it happened on an occasion when Jesus was teaching that "the power of the Lord was present to heal them" (Luke 5:17). I infer from this that the power of the Lord might *not* have been present for him to heal them.

On this occasion a man was brought to Jesus by some of his friends. He was palsied and unable to walk, so his friends brought him on a pallet but the crowds were so heavy, they had to let him down through the roof. Luke notes that Jesus "saw their faith." I take it to mean their faith was evident in what they were doing. But the response of Jesus is very revealing. Instead of saying "rise up and walk," he said, *"Man, thy sins are forgiven thee. "*

If the statement was intended to be provocative, Jesus was not disappointed. *"And the scribes and the Pharisees began to reason, saying, Who is this which speaketh blasphemies? Who can forgive sins, but God alone?"* And here is where he opens up the question:

> But when Jesus perceived their thoughts, he answering said unto them, What reason ye in your hearts? Whether is easier, to say, Thy sins be forgiven thee; or to say, Rise up and walk? But that ye may know that the Son of man hath power upon earth to forgive sins, (he said unto the sick of the palsy,) I say unto thee, Arise, and take up thy couch, and go into thine house. And immediately he rose up before them, and took up that whereon he lay, and departed to his own house, glorifying God. And they were all amazed,

and they glorified God, and were filled with fear,
saying, We have seen strange things to day (Luke
5:22-26).

Forgiveness is a real grace and a wonderful thing. But how can we *know* that we are forgiven if nothing is changed?

It is clear in this account as well as in the law that there is a nexus between sin and disease:

> *Wherefore it shall come to pass, if ye hearken to these*
> *judgments, and keep, and do them, that the LORD thy*
> *God shall keep unto thee the covenant and the mercy*
> *which he sware unto thy fathers: And he will love thee,*
> *and bless thee, and multiply thee: he will also bless the*
> *fruit of thy womb, and the fruit of thy land, thy corn,*
> *and thy wine, and thine oil, the increase of thy kine,*
> *and the flocks of thy sheep, in the land which he sware*
> *unto thy fathers to give thee. Thou shalt be blessed*
> *above all people: there shall not be male or female*
> *barren among you, or among your cattle. And the*
> *LORD will take away from thee all sickness, and will*
> *put none of the evil diseases of Egypt, which thou*
> *knowest, upon thee; but will lay them upon all them*
> *that hate thee (Deuteronomy 7:12-15).*

Jesus' disciples knew this and that is why they asked Jesus about the man born blind: "Master, who did sin, this man, or his parents, that he was born blind?" Jesus answered, *"Neither hath this man sinned, nor his parents: but that the works of God should be made manifest in him" (John 9:2-3).*

The mistake the disciples made was in assuming that the nexus between sin and disease is necessarily personal. It is not. But the connection is there, nonetheless. Even in the well known passage about anointing the sick for healing, the connection is clear, though conditional:

> *Is any sick among you? let him call for the elders of*
> *the church; and let them pray over him, anointing him*

with oil in the name of the Lord: And the prayer of faith shall save the sick, and the Lord shall raise him up; and if he have committed sins, they shall be forgiven him" (James 5:14-15).

In his first letter, Peter reaches way back to find another connection. Speaking of Christ's suffering he says, *"Who his own self bare our sins in his own body on the tree, that we, being dead to sins, should live unto righteousness: by whose stripes ye were healed. "* Where did Peter get this? From Isaiah.

He is despised and rejected of men; a man of sorrows, and acquainted with grief: and we hid as it were our faces from him; he was despised, and we esteemed him not. Surely he hath borne our griefs, and carried our sorrows: yet we did esteem him stricken, smitten of God, and afflicted. But he was wounded for our transgressions, he was bruised for our iniquities: the chastisement of our peace was upon him; and with his stripes we are healed. All we like sheep have gone astray; we have turned every one to his own way; and the LORD hath laid on him the iniquity of us all (Isaiah 53:3-6).

I used to wonder why Jesus had to suffer through that long night. I knew he had to die for my sins. Why couldn't they just have taken him out and killed him? After all, they didn't torture the animal sacrifices. They just killed them.

The answer seems to be that sickness and disease are the consequence and evidence of sin. And healing is the earnest of forgiveness and resurrection.

Does God still heal sick people? Let me ask the question another way: Does God still forgive people? Of course he does. He forgives, he heals. But in the grand sweep of things that God is doing, our flesh is of secondary importance. Our character and our faith mean much more to God.

15

How Jesus Saves

For I am the least of the apostles, that am not meet to be called an apostle, because I persecuted the church of God. But by the grace of God I am what I am: and his grace which was bestowed upon me was not in vain; but I laboured more abundantly than they all: yet not I, but the grace of God which was with me. [i]

It has been a while since I have seen a roadside sign trumpeting "Jesus Saves." I saw one painted on the side of a barn somewhere along Route 66 back when people still drove to California that way. I recall there was one high on top of a church in downtown Los Angeles. I have been a believer in Jesus as long as I can remember, and I surely consider myself a Christian, but I still wonder a little when I see one of those signs.

What I wonder about is the message these signs convey to the non-Christian folks who see them. Jesus saves from *what*? Jesus saves *for* what? I don't mean to criticize the signs, because they aren't intended to convey the entire Christian faith. And perhaps to a person whose life is coming apart, they are a beacon that shows them there just might be another, better way.

What started me thinking about this was the fine book by David Aikman, "A Man of Faith, The Spiritual Journey of George W. Bush." It is profoundly clear that for President Bush, becoming a Christian has been a rather long spiritual journey.

There have been people in the history of faith who have had a Damascus Road experience. Most don't. But because of the jargon used by so many religious people, not a few attempt to describe their conversion as a light from heaven, a moment that turned them around. In many cases, though, that one moment in their life was a long time coming and has still not ended.

What I found fascinating, and encouraging, is the fact that while George Bush has described himself as having accepted Christ as his personal Savior, and as being born again, the President and the White House stopped using those terms. What is encouraging to me, though is the *reason* they stopped. Reports were that they made the change to get away from the *jargon* that Christian people are accustomed to using among themselves and which are meaningless to outsiders.

Christians have, I think, hindered their efforts at evangelism by hiding their faith behind slogans like "Jesus saves," and by not explaining to people what that means.

For George Bush, there were many important moments. One was a conversation with the well known evangelist Arthur Blessit. [ii] Another was time spent with Billy Graham, who had a profound influence on his life. But no one really knows, perhaps not even George Bush himself, when the real turn came. Perhaps that is because the turn itself was so subtle and so early that no one noticed where it was leading. Not even George Bush himself.

But all of Bush's closest friends believe that the moment he changed from an "Assenting Believer" to a *follower of Christ* was his conversation with Billy Graham. Aikman describes an assenting believer as one who agrees with the Christian faith and at some level has expressed assent to it.

I fear that describes the religion of too many who consider themselves Christians. They are mere "believers." They are not followers. But what really struck me about Bush's spiritual journey, was that his moment of *real change* came entirely on his own. And it didn't come out of nowhere. It came from lifelong reading of the Bible, a remarkable persistence in pursuing Bible study, alone and with a community Bible Study Group. Like water wears away a stone, the persistent reading of the Bible sooner or later will wear a hole in a man's conscience.

The most dramatic moment for Bush came after a night when he and his friends had entirely too much to drink. He woke with a terrible hangover and wasn't able to complete his run. He made a decision while he was running to never drink again, and apparently has followed up with that decision. David Aikman describes the result this way:

> Every day for several years, his mind and spirit had been absorbing Christian truths from the Bible. But now, unencumbered by old, strong, alcohol induced habits, he was free to live out those truths far more powerfully than he must originally have imagined possible.

The change was revolutionary, and I think that is what so many Christians are trying to tell you when they say that "Jesus Saves." Their lives were coming apart and the decision, not merely to *believe* in Jesus, but to *follow* him, turned their lives around. Jesus made it very clear that far more than a different way of thinking was involved.

> *And why call ye me, Lord, Lord, and do not the things which I say? Whosoever cometh to me, and heareth my sayings, and doeth them, I will show you to whom he is like: He is like a man which built an house, and digged deep, and laid the foundation on a rock: and when the flood arose, the stream beat vehemently upon that house, and could not shake it: for it was founded upon a rock. But he that heareth, and doeth not, is like a man that without a foundation built an house upon the earth; against which the stream did beat vehemently, and immediately it fell; and the ruin of that house was great (Luke 6:46-49).*

George Bush himself said, "When you turn your heart and your life over to Christ, when you accept Christ as the Savior, it changes your heart, it changes your *life*. And that's what happened to me."

Yes, and it has happened to a lot of people. The fact is, evangelists don't save people. God does that. And it is rarely a singular experience that does the trick. All evangelists can do is to call your attention to God and to the reason why your life isn't working.

It is a long road along which the Spirit of God steers us to bring us to the place where we finally make the change. And what, exactly is that change? It is the moment when we make Jesus Christ our Master, and the Lord of our life. It is the day he becomes our Rabbi, our Teacher. It is the time when we begin to hang on his words and to direct our choices by those words.

Salvation is a miracle, but it is not magic. You might get the impression that it is magic to hear some people talk about it. Just give your hand to the preacher and your heart to the Lord and you are saved. Being saved means you will spend eternity in heaven instead of hell.

I'm sorry. It is not quite that simple, and Jesus told you it was not. When you give your hand to the preacher and join the church, you become an *assenting believer*. But when you make Jesus your Master, the process of salvation really begins.

The impression I gained from reading David Aikman's description of the President's spiritual journey is that what really made the difference was the consistent reading of the Bible. And it isn't just a New Testament thing. There are administrative differences between the administration of Moses and the administration of Jesus. But the underlying morality, the underlying truth, the underlying laws, are all the same.

I want to tell you a story about man who was saved. I want you to understand what his being saved actually meant. But first, there was another man we must understand. His name was Stephen. He was one of the first deacons of the fledgling church. He was something of a firebrand, and found himself in strong conflict with the Jewish leadership. Finally at the climax of one of his debates, he said to them:

Ye stiffnecked and uncircumcised in heart and ears,
ye do always resist the Holy Ghost: as your fathers
did, so do ye. Which of the prophets have not your

fathers persecuted? and they have slain them which showed before of the coming of the Just One; of whom ye have been now the betrayers and murderers: Who have received the law by the disposition of angels, and have not kept it (Acts 7:51-53).

There were few things Stephen could have said that would have angered them more. Blind with fury, they gnashed their teeth at him, dragged him outside the walls of the city and stoned him to death. Almost as an aside, Luke mentions that the witnesses (by law the witnesses or accusers had to cast the first stone) laid down their robes at the feet of a young man. His name was Saul.

The next thing we hear about Saul was that he was complicit in the death of Stephen and that he was one of the most aggressive persecutors of the fledgling church: *"As for Saul, he made havock of the church, entering into every house, and haling men and women committed them to prison."* Even in this, he was instrumental in spreading the Gospel because *"they that were scattered abroad went every where preaching the word" (Acts 8:3-4).*

The conversion of Saul has entered our language as a "Damascus Road experience." But what happened to Saul was much bigger than what happened to him on the road. He had set out on that journey *"breathing out threatenings and slaughter against the disciples of the Lord."* Saul was all but breathing fire about this new sect, which he considered a blasphemous sect of Judaism. He took the initiative to go to Damascus and to bring back, under arrest, any Christian disciples he found.

On the road, a light shined on him, so bright that it took him to the ground, and a voice came from the light thundering his name: *"Saul, Saul, why are you persecuting me?" (Acts 9:4).*

"Who are you, Lord," Saul asked, fearing the worst. *"I am Jesus whom you are persecuting,"* the voice replied. "It is hard for you to kick against the goads."

This last underlines a suspicion I have long had about Paul. His deep hatred for the Christian sect grew out of a heart filled with fear. He was afraid of the idea that Jesus might have actually been raised from the dead, because if that were true, then it would mean everything Jesus said against Paul's own particular set of beliefs had to be seriously considered. The very idea of Jesus was threatening beyond comprehension to the entire edifice of Paul's faith.

The Damascus Road experience was not Paul's moment of conversion. It was the moment that stopped him in his headlong rush to personal destruction. That moment of stopping is an important step in the process we describe as "Jesus Saves."

This experience was followed by three days of blindness during which he refused to eat or drink. No one can fully appreciate what those three days were like for Paul. He was devastated. His entire life lay around him in shambles. He needed those three days to sort through far too many things in his life, his way of thinking, his idea of truth.

He already knew a great deal about what Jesus said. No one with Paul's intellect and depth of hatred could fail to have fully examined the ideas he was opposing. Now he had to fit what he knew about Jesus into what he knew about the law, what he knew about Judaism, and what Jesus might have in store for him. He knew beyond doubt what he deserved. What he didn't know was what Jesus had in mind for him.

Meanwhile, there was a disciple of Jesus at Damascus named Ananias. The Lord spoke to him in vision, and said: *"Arise and go to the street called Straight, and inquire at the house of Judas for one called Saul of Tarsus, for behold, he is praying. And in a vision he has seen a man named Ananias coming in and putting his hand on him, so that he might receive his sight" (Acts 9:11-12).*

Now Ananias was no fool, and he had heard about Saul. But overriding his objections, God told him to go anyway and in the process revealed the mission he had in mind for Saul. Get on down there, said the Lord, "for he is a chosen vessel unto me, to bear my name before the Gentiles, and kings, and the children of Israel: For I will show him how great things he must suffer for my name's sake."

There is a terrible irony in that last statement. Saul had thought Christians needed to suffer, so the Lord was going to show Saul what suffering was really all about. And probably no disciple of Jesus in those years suffered any more than Saul was destined to suffer – even to death.

Few people have ever experienced as dramatic a conversion as Saul, but to tell the truth, Saul was still a long way from conversion on this day. The basic character of the man, his hostility, his temper, his adversarial approach to nearly everything, had not gone away. It was now redirected at a new set of objects. He so antagonized the Jews in the synagogues at Damascus, that they finally hatched a plot to kill him. The plot failed.

I don't believe for a moment that it was merely his persuasion and the proof that Jesus was the Christ that made these people want to kill him. I think it was the kind of adversary he naturally tended to be, and I think that is borne out by what happened later. He traveled back to Jerusalem, and when Barnabas introduced him to the church there, he followed the same practice in the synagogues there that he had followed in Damascus, with the same result. They had to get him out of town.

It wasn't the message of Saul that kept him in hot water. He heated the water himself. Most of the disciples managed to function, to preach and teach without getting themselves killed. But Stephen and Saul were rather more aggressive, even abrasive, in their approach than the others. After they shipped Saul off to his home town in Tarsus, *"Then had the churches rest throughout all Judaea and Galilee and Samaria, and were edified; and walking in the fear of the Lord, and in the comfort of the Holy Ghost, were multiplied" (Acts 9:31).*

And this last piece of the record underscores what I am trying to say. The innate hostility in Paul was not cured magically by his belief in Jesus. He had a long, hard road ahead of him. Remember what God told Ananias about Paul? *"For I will show him how great things he must suffer for my name's sake."* Saul, now called Paul, gives us a summary of that in his second Corinthian letter:

> *Are they ministers of Christ?; I speak as a fool; I am more: in labors more abundant, in stripes above measure, in prisons more frequently, in deaths often. From the Jews five times I received forty stripes minus one. Three times I was beaten with rods; once I was stoned; three times I was shipwrecked; a night and a day I have been in the deep; in journeys often, in perils of waters, in perils of robbers, in perils of my own countrymen, in perils of the Gentiles, in perils in*

> *the city, in perils in the wilderness, in perils in the sea, in perils among false brethren; in weariness and toil, in sleeplessness often, in hunger and thirst, in fastings often, in cold and nakedness; besides the other things, what comes upon me daily: my deep concern for all the churches (2 Corinthians 11:23-28).*

This was all a part of Paul's conversion process and it continued to the day he died. It was all quite fair. After all that Paul had done, he had some bitter lessons to learn. By the time he wrote the last letter of his life, 2 Timothy, we find a much more mellow man. A man who has managed to make peace with himself and with some people he had been at odds with.

And this is the message for you and me. Conversion, even salvation if you will, is a lifelong process. It is what David Aikman called a spiritual journey. It is the process of learning to live life by God's standards instead of your own. It is the process of learning to make life work for yourself and for others. What is the point in taking a man to the Kingdom whom others can't stand to be around?

---

i. 1 Corinthians 15:9-10.

ii. Arthur Blessit's claim to fame came from carrying a giant cross around the world.

16

The Hatred of God

He who hates Me hates My Father also.
If I had not done among them the works which no one else did,
they would have no sin; but now they have seen and also hated
both Me and My Father. But this happened that the word might be
fulfilled which is written in their law, "They hated Me without a
cause" (John 15:23-25 NKJV).

How could a man come to hate God? And why? At one level, it makes no sense. And yet real hatred of God festers in the world, a hatred of God that is visceral, primeval, strange, and irrational. Man doesn't *naturally* hate God, but still there are those who hate him. It is so fundamental that it finds a place very early in the Ten Commandments: *"I the LORD thy God am a jealous God, visiting the iniquity of the fathers upon the children unto the third and fourth generation of them that hate me" (Exodus 20:5).*

How strange it is that anyone would hate God personally. There are those who, while they know nothing of God, hate the very idea of God. There are those who want all mention of God eliminated from public life. They have managed to get the Ten Commandments removed from a courtroom. Sooner or later, they will go after the version that is on the wall at the Supreme Court. They have fought prayer of any kind in school. Even a moment of silence is troubling because it *implies* prayer. They have fought, not only the reading of the Bible in school, but even the presence of the Bible. A teacher was not allowed to have a closed Bible on his desk.

I will readily admit that not everyone who participates in these efforts actually *hates* God. In the 1950's there were hard core communists in this country, people who hated the United States and its form of government. Their work was made easier by what the communists called "useful idiots." In the same way, there are the people in our society who hate God and there are the useful idiots who help them.

Why is this happening? Why the fierce drive to ferret out every last vestige of religious observance from public life? It seems they have used everything except Bible sniffing dogs to get God out of the courts and out of the schools. How long before churches have to remove their signs from the public streets?

There is a war going on, but it is not a new thing. Paul spoke of this war in the first century. *"For though we walk in the flesh, "*he said, *"we do not war after the flesh: For the weapons of our warfare are not carnal, but mighty through God to the pulling down of strong holds" (2 Corinthians 10:3-4).*

The weapons of our warfare are not carnal – not "of the flesh." Paul went on to say, *"We demolish arguments and every pretension that sets itself up against the knowledge of God, and we take captive every thought to make it obedient to Christ. "* The constitutional arguments that are made on every side are pretexts. They are what Paul called "pretensions" that set themselves against the knowledge of God. Once you realize this and you start looking for the pretexts, they become all too obvious.

Why, for example, the irrational objection to a monument that merely memorialized the Ten Commandments? That's easy. The Seventh Commandment is *"Thou shalt not commit adultery, "* and sexual sin is the defining characteristic of our generation. But there's more. The Fourth Commandment dares to identify God. The critics are right who say the Ten Commandments are not about a generic god. The God of the Ten Commandments created the earth in six days and rested the seventh day. The God of the Ten Commandments has a name.

Perhaps even more important is the commandment that specifically addresses the hatred of God. *"Thou shalt not make unto thee any graven image, or any likeness of any thing that is in heaven above, or that is in the earth beneath, or that is in the water under the earth: Thou shalt not bow down thyself to them, nor serve them: for I the LORD thy God am a jealous God, visiting the iniquity of the fathers upon the children unto the third and fourth generation of them that hate me" (Exodus 20:4-5).*

This commandment is about more than pictures on a wall, or statues in the vestry. It is about the rejection of God in favor of an idol. It is about the hatred of God. This idea is developed further in the Psalms. God issues a warning against foreign gods, against the stubborn hearts of Israel and then adds this.

> *If my people would but listen to me, if Israel would follow my ways, how quickly would I subdue their enemies and turn my hand against their foes! Those who hate the Lord would cringe before him, and their punishment would last forever. But you would be fed with the finest of wheat; with honey from the rock I would satisfy you (Psalm 81:13-16 NIV).*

The word "hate" in Hebrew implies "to hate *personally.*" We think we would never fall for that, but a lot of otherwise good people have. Consider the Pharisees of Jesus' day. Here was a religious people, a people who considered themselves to be godly. They gave tithes of all they possessed. They fasted regularly. They were often in the Temple to worship God. They prayed in the streets and in the Temple.

And yet, they were a people eaten up with hostility. They were constantly in conflict, not only with the other Jewish sects of the day, but even among themselves. One of the first deacons in the early church found himself in conflict with them, and his judgment of them was harsh:

> *You stiff-necked people, with uncircumcised hearts and ears! You are just like your fathers: You always resist the Holy Spirit! Was there ever a prophet your fathers did not persecute? They even killed those who predicted the coming of the Righteous One. And now you have betrayed and murdered him – you who have received*

> *the law that was put into effect through angels but have not obeyed it (Acts 7:51-53 NIV).*

The Pharisees who got this tongue lashing were furious. You would think they could shrug their shoulders and dismiss Stephen as a madman. The problem was, Stephen had told them the truth about themselves. They could have handled anything else, but not this. They rushed him, and yelling at the top of their voices, they dragged him out of the city and stoned him to death.

What is this all about? Why this visceral hatred of this good man? People don't reserve this kind of hatred for fools. This kind of hatred only arises when people feel threatened in their innermost being.

Then there is the response of the mob to Jesus. The Lord was determined to challenge the restrictive rules the Pharisees had built up around the Sabbath day and his moment of choice was a healing in the synagogue on the Sabbath day. There was a man in attendance at this synagogue who had a withered hand and, since Jesus was known to heal the sick, they watched him to see whether he would heal the man on the Sabbath (See Mark 3:1 ff.).

Jesus framed his challenge carefully. He called for the man to stand and and then asked his question: *"Is it lawful to do good on the Sabbath days, or to do evil? to save life, or to kill?"* No one would answer, so Jesus told the man to stretch forth his hand. While everyone watched, the hand became whole just like the other. The response from those assembled? *"And the Pharisees went forth, and straightway took counsel with the Herodians against him, how they might destroy him."*

Why would they do that? Luke adds a descriptive phrase: "And they were filled with madness." Madness. A stupid, irrational rage. There is a fascinating Psalm that describes this deplorable spirit:

> *Hold not thy peace, O God of my praise; For the mouth of the wicked and the mouth of the deceitful are opened against me: they have spoken against me with a lying tongue. They compassed me about also with words of hatred; and fought against me without a cause (Psalm 109:1-3).*

This Psalm is widely attributed to David as a type of Christ. The Psalm even foreshadows Judas, one of the truly enigmatic figures in the Bible. What strange, convoluted motives stirred in that man to lead him to betray Jesus? David's prayer concerning the man who was a type of Judas is almost frightening. How bad does a person have to be for this punishment described in this Psalm to be just? [i]

No miracle of Jesus was more dramatic than the raising of Lazarus from the dead (John 11:43-53). From the moment Lazarus fell ill, Jesus knew. They sent people to tell him that Lazarus was sick, but Jesus delayed. The delay is the most puzzling aspect of this miracle, but it is also the most significant. It has been suggested that some held the belief that the spirit of a man hovered near the body for three days after his death. Resuscitation was not unknown. A man could appear to be dead who really was not. So they waited a while after death just to be sure.

Jesus wanted to make sure that everyone understood that he had power over death, power to give life. So he delayed until the three days had passed before he came to the place where Lazarus was buried. The two sisters of Lazarus were distraught, and so disappointed that Jesus had not come more quickly. It is a terribly poignant story, and it includes that shortest verse of the Bible, "Jesus wept."

Jesus went to the place where Lazarus was entombed, and in a moment of high drama, had them roll back the stone and called out, *"Lazarus, come forth."* And he who had been dead staggered out of the tomb still bound hand and foot with grave clothes. Anyone present would have been agape. But not all. Some gritted their teeth.

> *But some of them went their ways to the Pharisees, and told them what things Jesus had done. Then gathered the chief priests and the Pharisees a council, and said, What do we? for this man doeth many miracles. If we let him thus alone, all men will believe on him: and the Romans shall come and take away both our place and nation . . . Then from that day forth they took counsel together for to put him to death"* (John 11:46-53).

It would be one thing if we could stand aside from all this.

But we can't. Jesus made this clear at the Last Supper. He told his disciples this.

> *If the world hate you, ye know that it hated me before it hated you. If ye were of the world, the world would love his own: but because ye are not of the world, but I have chosen you out of the world, therefore the world hateth you. Remember the word that I said unto you, The servant is not greater than his lord. If they have persecuted me, they will also persecute you; if they have kept my saying, they will keep yours also. But all these things will they do unto you for my name's sake, because they know not him that sent me (John 15:18-21).*

The world will hate those who follow Jesus, but why? And why would they hate Jesus? *"This comes to pass,"* said Jesus, *"that the word might be fulfilled that is written in their law, They hated me without a cause" (John 15:25).*

But who are the people who hate Jesus "without a cause"? The government? The irreligious among us? No, Jesus went on to say, *"in fact, a time is coming when anyone who kills you will think he is offering a service to God" (John 16:2).*

Mel Gibson's movie, "The Passion" generated surprising passions of its own before it ever hit the theaters. It frightened some people, and that is perhaps as it should be. Because it is the story of man's hatred for God, and everything about God. The Passion of Jesus is, in fact, the climax of the story.

---

i. "Set thou a wicked man over him: and let Satan stand at his right hand. When he shall be judged, let him be condemned: and let his prayer become sin. Let his days be few; and let another take his office. Let his children be fatherless, and his wife a widow. Let his children be continually vagabonds, and beg: let them seek their bread also out of their desolate places. Let the extortioner catch all that he hath; and let the strangers spoil his labour. Let there be none to extend mercy unto him: neither let there be any to favour his fatherless children. Let his posterity be cut off; and in the generation following let their name be blotted out. Let the iniquity of his fathers be remembered with the LORD; and let not the sin of his mother be blotted out. Let them be before the LORD continually, that he may cut off the memory of them from the earth" (Psalm 109:6 ff.).

17

Talking with God

*Let the words of my mouth, and the meditation of my heart, be
acceptable in thy sight, O LORD, my strength, and my redeemer.*[i]

Seven Laws of Prayer

There is much that we don't understand about prayer, personal
or intercessory. Why does God answer one prayer and not another?
Why does God seem to prefer the small miracle to the big ones?
When a person survives a terrible accident, he thanks God for his
protection. But why didn't God just prevent the accident? After all,
we pray for his guidance and protection.

That said, there are some things we do know about prayer,
and they are generally much more important than the things we don't
know. I present for your consideration, seven immutable laws of
prayer.

Law number one: We all must die.

We can't change this rule. Adam and Eve might have eaten of
the Tree of Life and lived forever. That option is not open to us. Paul
wrote to the Hebrews, "It is appointed unto men once to die"
(Hebrews 9:27). King Solomon wrote, "To every thing there is a
season, and a time to every purpose under the heaven: A time to be

born, and a time to die" (Ecclesiastes 3:1-2).

No amount of prayer can change that. We may be able through prayer to postpone the evil day, but sooner or later we have to go. The Psalmist said that the years of man's life would be 70, or by reason of strength, 80. After that, he is living on borrowed time.

The most we can do in prayer, once we have come to the end of the road, is to ask for an extension as King Hezekiah did. He was, in the terms the Bible used, "sick unto death." God's word to him was to set his house in order. He would die and not live. It would have been a very unusual man who could have taken that message without begging for more. Hezekiah was not that man.

> *Then Hezekiah turned his face toward the wall, and prayed unto the LORD, And said, Remember now, O LORD, I beseech thee, how I have walked before thee in truth and with a perfect heart, and have done that which is good in thy sight. And Hezekiah wept sore. Then came the word of the LORD to Isaiah, saying, Go, and say to Hezekiah, Thus saith the LORD, the God of David thy father, I have heard thy prayer, I have seen thy tears: behold, I will add unto thy days fifteen years (Isaiah 38:2-5).*

Now you too can make that request, but you should know that the extra time gave Hezekiah a chance to make some serious mistakes. He might have been better off to accept God's judgment in the first place. It is worth knowing that God knows what is best for us at every stage of the game. Even Jesus, when asking that he be spared the death on the cross, asked that God's will be done, not his.

There is a corollary to the law that all men must die: Death is not the end. A man should prepare for the day of his death, in the terms of Isaiah, he should set his house in order. But in prayer, *we must look beyond death.*

We should remember that sometimes, in asking God to give a man more time, we are asking for more pain, more suffering and the chance of great loss. So, in prayer, never forget law number one. You and the person you are praying for are both going to die. What then?

Law number two: Prayer without works is vain.

I knew a man who once refused to go to the dentist. Instead, he prayed that God would heal his cavities. God never did. Now I can understand why he didn't want to go to the dentist. But I am not so sure about the *basis* of his prayer. Why should God heal your teeth when you can go to the dentist and get them fixed? You can't pray that God will prosper you and then refuse to go look for a job. You can't pray that God will bless your investments when you don't do your research. So why should he heal you when you don't do what you can?

Almost everyone can recite James' good advice about faith: "But wilt thou know, O vain man, that faith without works is dead?" (James 2:20). Citing the example of Abraham, Sarah, and even Rahab the Harlot, he concludes, "For as the body without the spirit is dead, so faith without works is dead also" (James 2:26).

You can't pray that God will heal your broken arm, then refuse to get it set, and expect God to do it for you. It's an old truism and all the better for age: God will not do for you what you can do for yourself.

So when you pray, ask God *and yourself* what you ought to be doing about this problem. Should you pray for the sick and then not visit them or write them or call them? Shouldn't you ask if there is anything you can do to help?

Law number three: You need help to pray.

This is true always and at all times. I take a great deal of heart from what Paul told the Romans about prayer. He said in the plainest terms, "we don't know what we should pray for as we ought" (Romans 8:26). The Spirit, he said helps us by making intercession for us "with groanings that cannot be uttered." The Spirit, Paul said, makes intercession for the saints *according to the will of God.* The Spirit knows things that we don't know, so the prayer for us can always be in God's will. Thus, "all things work together for good to them that love God, to them who are the called according to his purpose" (v. 28).

There are times when we are helpless, and distressingly often this happens at a time when we need prayer terribly. And we can't pray. At times like this, you have to ask for help. But what can you do? You *can* borrow the prayers of others. Why do you think these prayers are recorded in the Bible if not for you to use? I know, it may seem strange to merely recite a prayer, but that is not what I am suggesting. I am suggesting that you take the prayer from the Psalms and make it your own.

Law number four: You are God's servant. It is not the other way around.

You should not be asking God to get you a taxi. You should not be asking God to wait on your table. It is good to practice what is sometimes called, "the presence of God." It is good to be aware of God at all times, to be "instant in prayer," as Paul said. It is good to pray always and about everything. But don't get *presumptuous*. Persistence is good, but presumptuousness is not.

If you want to read an excellent example of how one can be persistent in prayer and yet not presume upon god, read the exchange between Abraham and God about the sparing of Sodom. God was on his way to see how bad things really were in Sodom when he stopped off to see Abraham. As God was ready to go on his way, he asked himself, "Shall I hide from Abraham what I am about to do?" He turned and told him that the cry of Sodom was so great that he was going to see for himself just how bad it was.

> *And Abraham drew near, and said, Wilt thou also destroy the righteous with the wicked? Peradventure there be fifty righteous within the city: wilt thou also destroy and not spare the place for the fifty righteous that are therein? That be far from thee to do after this manner, to slay the righteous with the wicked: and that the righteous should be as the wicked, that be far from thee: Shall not the Judge of all the earth do right? (Genesis 18:23-25).*

It really is a bold statement, considering the power differential between them, but God was not angry. He replied:

And the LORD said, If I find in Sodom fifty righteous within the city, then I will spare all the place for their sakes. And Abraham answered and said, Behold now, I have taken upon me to speak unto the Lord, which am but dust and ashes: Peradventure there shall lack five of the fifty righteous: wilt thou destroy all the city for lack of five? And he said, If I find there forty and five, I will not destroy it. And he spake unto him yet again, and said, Peradventure there shall be forty found there. And he said, I will not do it for forty's sake. And he said unto him, Oh let not the Lord be angry, and I will speak: Peradventure there shall thirty be found there. And he said, I will not do it, if I find thirty there. And he said, Behold now, I have taken upon me to speak unto the Lord: Peradventure there shall be twenty found there. And he said, I will not destroy it for twenty's sake. And he said, Oh let not the Lord be angry, and I will speak yet but this once: Peradventure ten shall be found there. And he said, I will not destroy it for ten's sake" (Genesis 18:26-32).

It becomes clear that we can reason with God. We can even plead our case and make our argument. But notice the *humility* of Abraham. Never does he presume upon God. He never forgot who was boss.

There is also a corollary to law number four: God doesn't have to explain himself to you and me. When Job was so far down it seemed he couldn't go any lower, he said this: "Though he slay me, yet will I trust in him: but I will maintain mine own ways before him. He also shall be my salvation: for an hypocrite shall not come before him" (Job 13:15-16).

Law number five: Absolute honesty is required. You have to tell the truth.

Don't pretend you love your enemy while you hate him in your heart. God knows, so you might as well own up to it. Some people have a problem with the vehemence of many of the Psalms.

Take this one, for example:

> *The wicked are estranged from the womb: they go astray as soon as they be born, speaking lies. Their poison is like the poison of a serpent: they are like the deaf adder that stoppeth her ear; Which will not hearken to the voice of charmers, charming never so wisely. Break their teeth, O God, in their mouth: break out the great teeth of the young lions, O LORD. Let them melt away as waters which run continually: when he bendeth his bow to shoot his arrows, let them be as cut in pieces. As a snail which melteth, let every one of them pass away: like the untimely birth of a woman, that they may not see the sun (Psalm 58:3-8).*

This is really a hard judgment he is asking for here. What ever happened to "love your enemies"? Should anyone pray like this? Well, notice that he doesn't mention any names here. He speaks of "the wicked" and describes what they do. For the people described here, the punishment is quite just.

Sometimes, you have to learn to love your enemies. It doesn't come naturally. And you can't start out by pretending that you love them. Some of the Psalms are pretty harsh, but they are painfully honest.

I learned this the easy way, once. I was praying about a man in the spirit of this Psalm. And as I tried to pray it, I found I couldn't. God's spirit would not allow me to curse the man. But because I was honest in my prayer, I found out what was not right in my own heart. You might as well be honest about what is in your heart. God knows it anyway.

Law number six: Prayer takes time and meditation.

If you are going to pray according to God's will, you are going to have to spend some time thinking about his will, and getting to know him. Thinking is a lost art. Most of us simply can't stand to be alone with our own thoughts. We have to listen to something, read something, say something to someone. But no, you really don't.

I will never forget an assignment that Dr. Jim Stark gave a group of us in management class. One week he had us keep a log of how we spent every 10 minutes of every day. The next week, he let us ease up to every 15 minutes, but then he added another requirement. We had to spend one hour in that week doing absolutely nothing but thinking. We could think about anything we wanted, including our job. But we couldn't do anything else while we did.

It was an absolutely revolutionary experience. I don't know if I had ever done that before. In the Bible, this is called meditation. Learn to be alone with yourself, and perhaps you can learn to be alone with God.

Law number seven: When it comes to words, more is not better.

> *Keep thy foot when thou goest to the house of God, and be more ready to hear, than to give the sacrifice of fools: for they consider not that they do evil. Be not rash with thy mouth, and let not thine heart be hasty to utter any thing before God: for God is in heaven, and thou upon earth: therefore let thy words be few. For a dream cometh through the multitude of business; and a fool's voice is known by multitude of words . . . For in the multitude of dreams and many words there are also divers vanities: but fear thou God (Ecclesiastes 5:1-7).*

I heard someone once urge his listeners to spend an hour a day in prayer. That's a good thing. I tried it. I put in the time, but I don't think there has ever been an occasion when I spent the whole time praying. My mind is just too active. I was all over the place, but I did manage to pray some of the time, and the exercise was good for me. And I learned that to spend time alone with God is holy time, *even when you say nothing at all.*

I remember a friend who once told me the reason why he liked to travel with a certain gentleman. He said, "We can be alone, side by side in the truck for a solid hour with neither of us saying a word. And it doesn't hurt his feelings a bit." I think I understand that.

I can be companionable with God while I say absolutely nothing. Some people can't bear silence. They think they have to fill it with words. They don't.

Now there was an occasion when Jesus spent all night in prayer. But I doubt seriously that he was talking the whole time. You don't have to actually be talking to be "in prayer."

> *Let the words of my mouth, and the meditation of my heart, be acceptable in thy sight, O LORD, my strength, and my redeemer (Psalm 19:14).*

Conclusion:

Being who I am, I get a lot of prayer requests, most from people I don't even know. And it is these prayer requests that made me stop and think about prayer, and about what people don't understand. It is painfully obvious, that people want prayers when life has gone sour. They ask for prayer reflexively. They say things like, "I need all the prayers I can get." Actually, you only need one.

> *Confess your faults one to another, and pray one for another, that ye may be healed. The effectual fervent prayer of a righteous man availeth much (James 5:16).*

You do know, don't you, that you can't work that up? I remember a little girl, she was eight if memory serves. She was hit by a truck out in front of her home. I was especially fond of that family, and I can tell you that I prayed fervently for that little girl. She died. I could say I don't know why she died, but I do. She died because she was hit by a truck and her injuries were beyond anything anyone could do.

That's not to say that God could not have healed her, but I don't think he has ever healed anyone whose body was so severely damaged. It occurs to me that the time to pray for the little girl is *before* she gets hit by a truck.

Thus we see seven immutable laws of prayer.

Law number one: We all must die.
Law number two: Prayer without works is vain.
Law number three: You need help to pray.
Law number four: You are God's servant. It is not the other way around.
Law number five: Absolute honesty is required.
Law number six: Prayer takes time and meditation.
Law number seven: When it comes to words, more is not better.

> *Be devoted to one another in brotherly love. Honor one another above yourselves. Never be lacking in zeal, but keep your spiritual fervor, serving the Lord. Be joyful in hope, patient in affliction, faithful in prayer. Share with God's people who are in need. Practice hospitality (Romans 12:10-13).*

---

i. *Psalms 19:14*

18

Close Encounters

I have heard of thee by the hearing of the ear:
but now mine eye seeth thee (Job 42:5).

After Job's long ordeal, and after his close encounter with God, he said something so profound that few have ever grasped it. He said, *"I have heard of thee by the hearing of the ear: but now mine eye seeth thee. "*

I can't help thinking that I *am* where Job *was*. I have heard of God with the hearing of the ear, but my eye has not seen him. Don't get me wrong. I believe in God, but so did Job. I obey God, but so did Job. I pray to God, but so did Job. There is no act of righteousness that I have done that Job would not have done. That means that I am squarely where Job was. And that means I very likely share his vulnerability.

I want to tell you where this first began to dawn on me and what I think it means. I was reading the fourth chapter of Revelation where John, in the manner of his day and time, is describing what he saw. He put all the events and players into a long paragraph, simply describing and summarizing all that he saw. John's account is a little confusing, so let me tell you how I think he saw it.

John fell into a vision. And in vision, he found himself in a place that was nothing like he had ever seen before. What dominated the scene was a throne with 24 seats arranged in a semicircle before it. There was a man seated on each of these seats with a golden crown on his head. John described them as elders.

Also before the throne, there were seven flames burning, which John describes as the seven spirits of God. And here, fool that I am, I thought there was only *one* Spirit of God. John also saw four creatures that were full of eyes before and behind. It seems kind of creepy, but don't lose track of the fact that this is a vision. As John watched, the creatures sang out: Holy, holy, holy, Lord God Almighty, which was, and is, and is to come.

Immediately, out of the throne there appeared lightning and a crack of thunder and there appeared on the throne, one whom John could only describe in terms of precious stones. Around him there appeared a greenish halo. Instantly, the 24 elders threw down their crowns and sang out: "Thou art worthy, O Lord, to receive glory and honour and power: for thou hast created all things, and for thy pleasure they are and were created." And then they threw themselves down before him who sat on the throne.

What I wondered as I read this account and tried to visualize it, was what went through the minds of the 24 elders as they did this? Was one of them thinking to himself, "Let's see, was I to sing this song and then throw down my crown, or was I to throw down the crown and then sing? Should I assume that they followed an order of service?

I don't think so. How could anyone who wears a crown, a legitimate symbol of power and authority, wear that crown in the presence of the great King of all the Universe? I think they did what was the most natural thing to do. They threw down their crowns, shouted praise to God and fell down before him. They needed no script. No order of service.

They did not do this because they were supposed to. They did not do it because they were commanded to do it. They did not do it out of a sense of obligation or duty. They did not do it following some accepted form. They did it because they couldn't do anything else. They did it because they saw with their eyes, the God of glory, and were simply overwhelmed.

And then I thought about poor Job who, even when he said he had now seen God at last, still had not seen what John saw. And I think about you and me and the simple fact that we have not even experienced what Job saw. We go to church because it is the thing to do. We sing hymns because we are supposed to. We pray because we are commanded to. We kneel in prayer, not so much out of respect and awe as out of custom. We worship on the Sabbath because it is the law. We go through the motions, shuffling our feet along the ground, never thinking to look up. But how could it be otherwise, seeing we have never had a close encounter with God?

We have another example. Like us, David never had a close encounter with God. Here was a man after God's own heart, yet God never spoke to him directly. He communicated with David through his friend and confidant, Nathan. The result of this relationship was a longing for God that found expression in the songs David wrote.

> *As the deer panteth after the water brooks,*
> *so panteth my soul after thee, O God.*
> *My soul thirsteth for God, for the living God:*
> *when shall I come and appear before God?*
> *My tears have been my food day and night,*
> *while they continually say unto me, Where is thy God?*
>
> *When I remember these things, I pour out my soul in me:*
> *for I had gone with the multitude,*
> *I went with them to the house of God,*
> *with the voice of joy and praise,*
> *with a multitude that kept holyday.*
>
> *Why art thou cast down,*
> *O my soul? and why art thou disquieted in me?*
> *hope thou in God:*
> *for I shall yet praise him for the help of his countenance*
> *(Psalm 42).*

When a person knows that God is there, but he can't touch him, can't see him, there *should* be a longing for God. Unless, of course, God is not in his thoughts. Then, a man can walk through life with no awareness of God, no sense of God's presence, no awareness of the closeness of God.

But when we are far away from God, whose fault is that? Has

God left us, or have we just forgotten him? What you need to look for in yourself is not so much the presence of God, but the longing for God. When that returns, you know you are not in the right place, and never will be until you are with him.

Think about Job. When he was away from God, even though obedient, he was self-righteous. He assumed he had arrived. He assumed he had the right stuff. David never made that mistake. He never *assumed* his righteousness. But he did assume the closeness of God. Nowhere is this better expressed than in his 23rd Psalm.

> *The LORD is my shepherd; I shall not want.*
> *He maketh me to lie down in green pastures:*
> *he leadeth me beside the still waters.*
> *He restoreth my soul:*
> *He leadeth me in the paths of righteousness*
> *for his name's sake.*
> *Yea, though I walk through the valley*
> *of the shadow of death, I will fear no evil:*
> *for thou art with me; thy rod and thy staff they comfort me.*
> *Thou preparest a table before me*
> *in the presence of mine enemies:*
> *thou anointest my head with oil; my cup runneth over.*
> *Surely goodness and mercy*
> *shall follow me all the days of my life:*
> *and I will dwell in the house of the LORD for ever.*

But don't our sins separate us from God? Don't they make it impossible for us to approach him? Yes and no. Isaiah, as a very young man, had a close encounter with God. He describes what happened in the sixth chapter of his book.

In vision, he saw the Lord sitting on a throne, much as John would later see it. He notes that the throne is high and lifted up. He describes seraphs who fly and sing "Holy, holy, holy, is the LORD of hosts: the whole earth is full of his glory." The pillars of the door moved at the sound of the singing and the whole house was filled with smoke.

"Woe is me," said Isaiah, "for I am undone; because I am a man of unclean lips, and I dwell in the midst of a people of unclean lips: for mine eyes have seen the King, the LORD of hosts." Knowing he was a sinner, he knew he could not survive a close encounter with God. But then something marvelous happened.

> *Then flew one of the seraphims unto me, having a live*
> *coal in his hand, which he had taken with the tongs*
> *from off the altar: And he laid it upon my mouth, and*
> *said, "Lo, this hath touched thy lips; and thine iniquity*
> *is taken away, and thy sin purged" (Isaiah 6:6-7).*

Can it be that easy? Well, it is hardly easy. This is fire touching his lips. Yes, Christ's sacrifice covers all your sins, but the fire purifies and the pain causes us to draw near to God, to realize our dependence on him.

Once this issue was settled, Isaiah then heard a voice saying, "Whom shall I send, and who will go for us?" Now, Isaiah replies, "Here am I; send me."

Jacob was another man who had a close encounter with God. It is a strange instance in many ways, because it runs counter to our expectations of God.

> *And Jacob was left alone; and there wrestled a man*
> *with him until the breaking of the day. And when he*
> *saw that he prevailed not against him, he touched the*
> *hollow of his thigh; and the hollow of Jacob's thigh*
> *was out of joint, as he wrestled with him (Genesis*
> *32:24,25).*

It will become clear that Jacob was wrestling with God. Why God even bothered is an interesting question all by itself.

> *And the man said, Let me go, for the day breaketh.*
> *And he said, I will not let thee go, except thou bless*
> *me. And he said unto him, What is thy name? And he*
> *said, Jacob. And he said, Thy name shall be called no*
> *more Jacob, but Israel: for as a prince hast thou*
> *power with God and with men, and hast prevailed.*

No loser, this man. Jacob was a winner and an example of boldness with God.

> *And Jacob asked him, and said, Tell me, I pray thee, thy name. And he said, Wherefore is it that thou dost ask after my name? And he blessed him there. And Jacob called the name of the place Peniel: for I have seen God face to face, and my life is preserved. And as he passed over Penuel the sun rose upon him, and he halted upon his thigh.*

So now we know. Jacob grappled all night with God and he won. What you should not forget, though, is that if indeed you have prevailed with God, perhaps if you ever do prevail with him, you also will have a limp or something like it. You will surely never be the same again.

So we go through our lives, going through the motions. We do our duty. We carry out our obligations. We do what we are supposed to do. And yet, we still seem to be far away from him. We have little sense of the immediacy of God. But there is one important thing to remember. The distance is not his doing, it is ours. And in truth, the distance is in our minds, not his. In my life, I have had reason to grasp the truth of what Paul said about this.

> *Likewise the Spirit also helpeth our infirmities: for we know not what we should pray for as we ought: but the Spirit itself maketh intercession for us with groanings which cannot be uttered. And he that searcheth the hearts knoweth what is the mind of the Spirit, because he maketh intercession for the saints according to the will of God. And we know that all things work together for good to them that love God, to them who are the called according to his purpose (Romans 8:26-28).*

I know that there have been times in my life when my prayer was either not working or nonexistent. But the Spirit was working, and God was with me even though I didn't realize he was there.

Why is God not more immediate in our lives and in our thoughts? Perhaps because in our heart of hearts we really don't want him there. We surely wouldn't want him there if we were surfing the Internet looking for pornography. We wouldn't want to think of God nearby if we are lying to our neighbor, or if we are visiting our neighbor's wife when he is away. But these things may not be our greatest danger. I fear many are unaware of that danger because they are just too well off. Life seems to be working, for now.

The warning is clear in Moses' sermon to Israel outlining what God expected of them. It shall be, Moses warned, when the Lord has brought you into a wonderful land, with great cities, great farms, plenty of water, when you have eaten and are full, *"Then beware lest you forget the Lord who brought you forth out of the land of Egypt, from the house of bondage" (Deuteronomy 6:12).*

It is the forgetting that kills us. It isn't so much the sin of weakness. It isn't so much the temptation of the devil and the world. It is the forgetting that would finally deny us our day of a close encounter with the Great and Holy One who is introduced by angels.

But when we forget, we don't realize it at the time. Only when the smoke alarm goes off do we realize we forgot and left the pan on the burner. The remedy must come before the forgetting, not after.

> *These commandments that I give you today are to be upon your hearts. Impress them on your children. Talk about them when you sit at home and when you walk along the road, when you lie down and when you get up. Tie them as symbols on your hands and bind them on your foreheads. Write them on the doorframes of your houses and on your gates (Deuteronomy 6:6-9 NIV).*

19

Disappointed with God

Why standest thou afar off, O LORD?
why hidest thou thyself in times of trouble? (Psalm 10:1 KJV)

God so often disappoints us. No, let's not kid ourselves, we place our hopes in God and those hopes are all too often disappointed. The fault, however, is not with God. The fault is with our expectations, and with what I call, "the God of our imagination." The only reason we could ever be disappointed with God is if He somehow doesn't meet *our* expectations.

Recently, someone reminded me of something I said in a sermon long ago and had all but forgotten. A great lady whom we all loved and for whom we had prayed long and hard, had died in pain from what was probably colon cancer. There was no small amount of disappointment when she died after so much prayer. My sermon addressed the basis of our disappointment. Rather bluntly, I fear, I said that God's objective in calling us is not merely to save our miserable hides, but to spend us in his service.

Specifically I said, "God is not in the business of the preservation and perpetuation of human flesh." And I think it is in this error that we so often become disappointed. We think our aches and pains are as important to God as they are to us. They may be, but it will not be for the same reason at all.

There was a man who is mentor to so many of us. His name was Saul of Tarsus. We have come to know him as the great Apostle

Paul. At one point in his ministry he was moved to write of his experiences with God. He said that he knew a man in Christ who had been caught up into paradise and heard unspeakable words, words which are not permitted man to utter. In context, it is clear that Paul himself was that man, but he doesn't want to couch it in those terms. And he is somewhat afraid of the consequences of that visit to paradise, because there was a very real danger there. He said:

> *And lest I should be exalted above measure, there was given to me a thorn in the flesh, the messenger of Satan to buffet me. Three times I pleaded with the Lord to take it away from me. But he said to me, "My grace is sufficient for you, for my power is made perfect in weakness" (2 Corinthians 12:7-9).*

Paul went on to say what his infirmities meant to him: *"Therefore I take pleasure in infirmities, in reproaches, in necessities, in persecutions, in distresses for Christ's sake: for when I am weak, then am I strong."*

I must confess I am not there yet. I can't take pleasure in my infirmities. Sometimes they hurt terribly. But I do understand what Paul means when he says, *"when I am weak, then I am strong."* That, I have experienced. Paul knew that he could not do what he did, that he could not know what he knew, go where he had gone, understand what he understood, and be whole in the flesh at the same time.

I can say this from Scripture, and I can confirm in my own life and experience. The greater the gifts from God, the closer one is to God, the more one understands of God, the more God intends to use a person in his service, the greater the *need* for infirmity of the flesh.

God so often disappoints us because he is so often subtle. We want to see the withered hand go straight right in front of our eyes. We want to watch as the man born blind can now see. We want to watch the man who had been crippled all his life now dance and laugh. We want to see Lazarus walk out of the tomb. We want to see fire fall down out of heaven. And we are a little bit disappointed when we don't see anything at all.

Actually, it is not that we don't see anything. God may make a sick man well, but we wonder if he just got better. He may find you a job, but you can't tell if he really did or if the job was just there, and time and chance led you to it. And that leads us inexorably to a fact of life: God is subtle in his dealings with man and he prefers to keep it that way. There has to be a reason for that.

Consider, for example, a man named Naaman. This man was not a Jew, but a Syrian of some importance. He was the military chief of staff to the King of Syria. But he was also a leper. As the story goes, he was an admirable man in spite of his leprosy, or perhaps because of it. A man with the kind of power he held could easily have been a very different man.

His wife had a servant, a little girl, who was a captive from Israel. She seems to have cared about this man, because she said to her mistress, *"Would God my lord were with the prophet that is in Samaria! for he would recover him of his leprosy"* (2 Kings 5:3).

Naaman heard of this, and when he spoke to the king, the response was immediate: *"Go, and I will send a letter unto the king of Israel."* Now this is impressive. It gives you some idea of the esteem the King of Syria held for Naaman. This was no ordinary general.

As the story develops, it has its amusing moments. When Naaman brought the letter to the King of Israel, it frightened him. He tore his clothes and said, *"Am I God, to kill and to make alive, that this man doth send unto me to recover a man of his leprosy? wherefore consider, I pray you, and see how he seeketh a quarrel against me."* That sort of gambit was not unheard of, and he feared an impending invasion.

But the Prophet Elisha heard of these goings on and called for the king to send Naaman down so he could learn that there really was a Prophet in Israel. So Naaman went, and stood at the door of Elisha's house with all his retinue. Elisha didn't even come to the door. He sent a servant out who spoke to Naaman and told him to go wash seven times in the Jordan River and he would be healed of his leprosy.

This did not go down well. It is fair to say that Naaman was disappointed. To put it mildly, he was furious. *"Behold, I thought, He will surely come out to me, and stand, and call on the name of the LORD his God, and strike his hand over the place, and recover the leper."* He wanted to see Elisha clap his hands and shout, "Be healed!" He didn't get it.

And so he went away in a rage muttering to himself, *"Are not the rivers of Damascus better than all the waters of Israel? May I not wash in them, and be clean?"* He had not come all this distance to take a bath in the Jordan.

But cooler heads came forward. His servant approached him and said, *"My father, if the prophet had bid thee do some great thing, wouldest thou not have done it? how much rather then, when he saith to thee, Wash, and be clean?"*

"Well, why not?" thought Naaman after a moment. So he went down to the river and immersed himself seven times, probably feeling like a fool as he counted off the first six times. But the seventh time, he came up with flesh as clear and clean as a small child.

We mustn't be disappointed with the subtlety of God. I think he enjoys it. He may even have laughed when he saw Naaman's face. And all this was set in motion by the words of *a little girl*. We would be well advised to get with the program and work God's way instead of ours.

Sadly, that is not the end of the story. Naaman returned to Elisha, and said, *"Behold, now I know that there is no God in all the earth, but in Israel: now therefore, I pray thee, take a blessing of thy servant."* He wanted to give him something, but Elisha refused. Gehazi, Elisha's servant saw this and felt it wasn't right. Elisha should have taken something from the man. He concocted a story, ran after Naaman and came home a richer man.

I suppose it is fair to say that Gehazi was disappointed in how God handled this. But it would seem that God was disappointed in Gehazi. When he returned and went in to his master, Elisha asked, *"Where have you been, Gehazi?"*

Gehazi lied, *"Your servant went no where."* And so Elisha made it clear that he knew exactly what had happened and then he made this point:

> *Is it a time to receive money, and to receive garments, and oliveyards, and vineyards, and sheep, and oxen, and menservants, and maidservants? The leprosy therefore of Naaman shall cleave unto thee, and unto thy seed for ever. And he went out from his presence a leper as white as snow (1 Kings 5:26-27).*

For his own reasons, God wanted to make this simple and to make a point while he was doing it. Taking money in exchange for healing corrupted the entire process and the lesson was lost. In an odd sense, the obligation this placed on Naaman, and his awe of the Israelite God was compromised.

It is so easy to be disappointed with God. Take Elijah as another example. He had seen the fire fall from heaven on Mount Carmel, and one would think he would have been the king of the hill after this. But in a matter of hours, he was fleeing for his life from Jezebel, who had long since proved she was capable of murder. Elijah fled south to get away and came to a place in the wilderness where he sat, exhausted and defeated in the meager shade of a juniper tree. He prayed, *"It is enough; now, O LORD, take away my life; for I am not better than my fathers" (1 Kings 19:4).*

But God was not finished with Elijah. An angel came and woke him, fed him and sent him on to Mount Horeb where he came to a cave and waited there. As he waited, the Lord came to him and asked, *"What are you doing here, Elijah?"* The reply from Elijah contains a whiff of self pity: *"I have been very jealous for the LORD God of hosts: for the children of Israel have forsaken thy covenant, thrown down thine altars, and slain thy prophets with the sword; and I, even I only, am left; and they seek my life, to take it away."*

> *"Go out,"* replied God, *"and stand upon the mountain before me."*

> *And, behold, the LORD passed by, and a great and strong wind rent the mountains, and brake in pieces the rocks before the LORD; but the LORD was not in the wind: and after the wind an earthquake; but the LORD was not in the earthquake: And after the earthquake a fire; but the LORD was not in the fire: and after the fire a still small voice.*

The subtle God then clarified the issues for Elijah. He gave him a couple of jobs to do and then said, By the way, you aren't really the only one left. *"Yet I have left me seven thousand in Israel, all the knees which have not bowed unto Baal, and every mouth which hath not kissed him" (1 Kings 19:18).*

We mustn't be disappointed with the subtlety of God. More often than not, it is his preferred manner of operation. And if we watch for it, we will be far more likely to see it when it comes. When we pray, we may not have the faith to move mountains. We may not be able to pray in faith that God will make the tumor just disappear (although he has done so). But we can pray for relief from pain. A good night's sleep. A better doctor. Better medication.

When you pray, look for that which God may do with subtlety. Look for the leadership of the Spirit in prayer. And expect the play to be subtle. You want to see the lame rise up and walk. That is great if it is God's moment for it. But it is disappointing if it is not.

Then, there was Jesus in the Garden of Gethsemane. Given many of the assumptions we might carry about Jesus, the account of this night could be disappointing. For Jesus asked his Father if there was any other way to do this. *"Is it possible that I might not have to drink of this cup?"* I suppose it is possible that Jesus could have decided even this late not to go through with it. All this might be disappointing if it were not for one thing. Jesus was prepared to go wherever God took him.

So what was God's answer? There was no clap of thunder, no lighting, no light from heaven. There was one subtle thing:

> *And he was withdrawn from them about a stone's cast, and kneeled down, and prayed, Saying, Father, if thou be willing, remove this cup from me: nevertheless not my will, but thine, be done. And there appeared an angel unto him from heaven, strengthening him (Luke 22:41-43).*

There was one other very important thing. Jesus adapted his hopes to the plan and the method. We are too often disappointed and discouraged because we fail to make that adaptation.

Now I don't want you to think we shouldn't ask God for the Big Event. By all means, ask God for the big stuff. He says you have not because you ask not. But at the same time, look for the subtlety of God, and join him in winning the fight before the enemy even knows there is one.

There was an occasion in Israel's early history when they were terribly oppressed by the Midianites. One day a man named Gideon was threshing wheat when a stranger came along and sat down in the shade near him. The man spoke, *"The Lord is with you, O mighty man of valor. "*

To tell the truth, I don't think Gideon immediately knew who he was talking to. He was puzzled, because he thought very little of himself – an important item in the story. I won't bore you with the whole story because it has been all but worn out by preachers over the years. But I recommend you read it again, starting in Judges 6, because it is a very endearing story regarding this faithful man.

Following instructions, Gideon sent word out to gather an army and he got a good one – 32,000 men in all. Now consider what God considers. That gang of Midianites was even bigger. They covered the ground like a plague of grasshoppers. We can arm our 32,000 men and charge into the valley and whip all those people, but a lot of good men will die in the process. In hand to hand combat, half the people on the field will probably die the first hour, half of the remainder the second hour.

So what shall we do? The first step was hardly what one would expect. God said, *"We have to cut this army down in size. "* I don't dare let this gang whip the Midianites lest they get too big for their britches (however God might say that). Walking through steps that included sending everyone home who was afraid, God whittled Gideon's force down to 300 men. In doing so, God lowers drastically the possible loss of life, and that's a good thing.

Then comes the tactical problem. The battalion was divided into three companies, each man armed with a trumpet, a lamp, and a pitcher. What the men were to do was occupy the surrounding hills. On a signal, every man blew his trumpet, broke the pitcher to display the light, and yelled at the top of his voice, *"The Sword of the Lord and of Gideon. "*

Taken completely by surprise, the Midianites fell over one another getting out of the valley. It was a subtle, but brilliant strategy. Normally, one man would have the trumpet to summon, say a thousand. The lamp served the purpose a banner would serve in the daytime – to locate the leader. For all the Midianites knew, they were surrounded by 300,000 men. Maybe more.

It is much better for us to get on God's wavelength, to think as he thinks, to see as he sees. A frontal assault is, in some cases, what's called for. But in other cases, he wants us to be as subtle as he is. This is what Jesus was telling his disciples when he said, *"Behold, I send you forth as sheep in the midst of wolves: be ye therefore wise as serpents, and harmless as doves" (Matthew 10:16).*

"We are saved by hope," said Paul.

> *But hope that is seen is not hope: for what a man seeth, why doth he yet hope for? But if we hope for that we see not, then do we with patience wait for it. Likewise the Spirit also helpeth our infirmities: for we know not what we should pray for as we ought: but the Spirit itself maketh intercession for us with groanings which cannot be uttered (Romans 8:24-26).*

Make your requests known to God. Ask as big as you want. But expect God to be subtle in his reply, because he is that way far more often than not. And if you are watching for God to be subtle, you are more likely to see his hand.

Oh, and one more thing. Don't forget to be thankful for it.

20

Taking Faith for Granted

See that ye refuse not him that speaketh.
For if they escaped not who refused him that spake on earth,
much more shall not we escape,
if we turn away from him that speaketh from heaven. [i]

Is faith something we can take for granted? Or is it like a lot of married couples? We have been together so long, we can complete sentences for one another. We can take one another for granted, and at some level, that is good. I can take it for granted that my wife will be faithful to me. I can take it for granted that she won't bust the budget. I do not even need to check on her credit card purchases. The only reason I look at them is to be sure there is no fraud. After 52 years of marriage, there aren't a lot of surprises, nor should there be.

At the same time, love calls on us to be *attentive* to one another. And this is where we too often fall down. Sometimes, we just don't listen when our mate talks to us. Sometimes we just go on doing whatever it is we are doing, and pay attention with half our mind. That isn't anything to become upset about, but it is wise to do something about it. We sometimes have to tell our loved one outright, "I need you for something, right now."

Now I want us to take a step forward from this and ask if we take our faith for granted in much the same way. A man and his wife can drive down a highway together and not say anything for an hour, but it is still good to be there together. Likewise, it may not be needful to speak to God every five minutes, but it is good to know he is there.

There is a problem, though, lurking in the background. We can wend our way through life taking God for granted. Why should I ask him to protect my job for me? I know he will. Why should I ask him to protect my life on this journey? I know he will. It is like a marriage in this way. Often, when we ask God, "Will you?" his answer is "Of course." But it is still good to ask, isn't it?

Wives really would be happier if their husbands were mind readers. They are thrilled when we think of something on our own that needs to be done. But wives more often have to ask. On the other hand, God may really *be* a mind reader, but apparently, he still wants us to ask.

But here also lies a paradox. When I come to a crossroads in my life, a decision I have to make, and I have a clear principle in the Bible as to what I ought to do, is it necessary to ask God to show me what to do? Or do I weary God, asking nonsensical questions? It is possible to weary God, you know. In an encounter with King Ahaz, Isaiah challenged him, *"Is it a small thing for you to weary men, but will ye weary my God also?" (Isaiah 7:13).*

Now God doesn't get tired, and that is not the sense of the word here. If I come to a point of annoyance where I say, "I am getting weary of this nonsense," you would know what I mean. God doesn't get tired, but he can become piqued with men. That is *not* the result I want.

It should not be surprising to learn that God is not impressed with words, especially a lot of words. In old times, it was customary to go up to the Temple to pray – there was even an hour of prayer, and Peter and the other disciples would go there at that time.[ii] But even then, there is a caution. The warning comes from Solomon who called mere words, "the sacrifice of fools."

Watch your step when you go to the house of God, he said, and be more ready to hear than to talk. Don't be in such a hurry to speak, *"for God is in heaven, and thou upon earth: therefore let thy words be few. For a dream cometh through the multitude of business; and a fool's voice is known by multitude of words" (Ecclesiastes 5:2-3).*

Now even between two people who have been married for fifty years, it is just as possible to have too much to say as too little. Not surprisingly, Jesus seems to be of the same mind as Solomon when it came to long prayers.

And when thou prayest, thou shalt not be as the hypocrites are: for they love to pray standing in the synagogues and in the corners of the streets, that they may be seen of men. Verily I say unto you, They have their reward. But thou, when thou prayest, enter into thy closet, and when thou hast shut thy door, pray to thy Father which is in secret; and thy Father which seeth in secret shall reward thee openly. But when ye pray, use not vain repetitions, as the heathen do: for they think that they shall be heard for their much speaking. Be not ye therefore like unto them: for your Father knoweth what things ye have need of, before ye ask him (Matthew 6:5-8).

Again the analogy with marriage presents itself. Often one partner will know what the other needs before the other one asks. Then Jesus continued with the familiar "Lord's prayer," a model of brevity and simplicity. It is not there for vain repetition, but as an example of prayer.

In Solomon's famous "*To every thing there is a season, and a time to every purpose under the heaven,*" he includes a caution that there is "*a time to keep silence, and a time to speak.*" It is true in marriage. It is true in the family of God. There is a time to speak and a time to shut up and go do what you know you should do.

I learned this lesson by experience, since I couldn't seem to learn it otherwise. When I got to the place where I had to leave a church I had served for 17 years, I just didn't want to make the decision. I prayed long and hard about it. Strange as it sounds, what I really wanted to happen was for the church to fire me so I wouldn't have to decide. Here is something to think about long and hard. When you want God to decide something for you, what you may be doing is trying to evade the *responsibility* for the decision. One day, as I was praying that God would show me what to do, the answer came clear.

There was no voice, but I suddenly realized that God had shown me all I needed to know, and all that he was going to show me. What he wanted from me was a decision. *He wanted me to accept the responsibility for what had to be done.* I knew what I should do. I just didn't want to carry the burden.

Something like this can happen in a marriage too. We would like to shove responsibility off on our partner. Leadership is good, but there is such a thing as too much leadership, because it can shut out the person being led and relieve them of responsibility.

I am digressing, but this is strongly related. I have heard people speak of empowering the membership of the church. The problem with this idea is that it assumes you have power to give and that means you are still in control. The real challenge is not to empower people, but to avoid relieving people of the responsibility that is theirs by right and necessity. Sometimes you have to refuse to lead in order to leave the door open for others to act. There is one thing you can take for granted. God will do very little that relieves you of the responsibility for making decisions and acting on them.

I have the distinct impression that God has a stark aversion to meddling in our affairs. That does not mean he is not interested. It means he is very interested in how we handle the challenge, for God is playing for very high stakes here. He isn't looking for specimens for his zoo. He isn't looking for automatons that, while they do as they are told, can't do anything more. He isn't looking for slaves, though we may describe ourselves as his bond servants. He is looking for Sons.

You can take that for granted, but that takes us to the other side of this question. We can take God for granted, but do we dare take our *faith* for granted?

"Let us labor, therefore," said Paul, *"to enter into that rest, lest any man fall after the same example of unbelief"* (Hebrews 4:11). He went on to say that the Word of God is powerful and sharp, and that *"Nothing in all creation is hidden from God's sight. Everything is uncovered and laid bare before the eyes of him to whom we must give account."* It is that rendering of an account that should give us pause.

The great Apostle goes on later in the book to urge us to pursue holiness, without which we can't hope to see God, and warns against failing of the grace of God.

See to it that you do not refuse him who speaks. If they did not escape when they refused him who warned them on earth, how much less will we, if we turn away from him who warns us from heaven? At that time his voice shook the earth, but now he has promised, "Once more I will shake not only the earth but also the heavens." The words "once more" indicate the removing of what can be shaken – that is, created things – so that what cannot be shaken may remain. Therefore, since we are receiving a kingdom that cannot be shaken, let us be thankful, and so worship God acceptably with reverence and awe, for our "God is a consuming fire" (Hebrews 12:25-29 NIV).

We can't afford to take our faith for granted. But how do we avoid that? The answer is simplicity itself. We *practice* our faith. We do the things that a man of faith should do. For example, the Bible says we can eat nearly anything that is called food, but then gives us a list of exceptions.[iii] We eat the things that are permitted, and we avoid the things that are not. This is a simple way to practice your faith. Another way we practice our faith is to keep the Sabbath.

If you refrain from trampling the sabbath, from pursuing your own interests on my holy day; if you call the sabbath a delight and the holy day of the LORD honorable; if you honor it, not going your own ways, serving your own interests, or pursuing your own affairs; then you shall take delight in the LORD, and I will make you ride upon the heights of the earth; I will feed you with the heritage of your ancestor Jacob, for the mouth of the LORD has spoken (Isaiah 58:13-14 NRSV).

Returning to God a tenth of whatever he gives you is still another way you practice your faith.

Woe unto you, scribes and Pharisees, hypocrites! for ye pay tithe of mint and anise and cummin, and have

> *omitted the weightier matters of the law, judgment,*
> *mercy, and faith: these ought ye to have done, and not*
> *to leave the other undone (Matthew 23:23).*

There are other ways just as important. Jesus offered three parables about his coming and the judgment of that day (See Matthew 25:1 ff.). The third of these three parables is about works of charity. When the Son of God returns in all his glory, he divides the nations before him into two camps. To the one he says, *"Come, ye blessed of my Father, inherit the kingdom prepared for you from the foundation of the world. "*Then he begins to recount the reasons for their reward. *"For I was hungry, "* he said, *" and you gave me something to eat. I was thirsty, and you gave me something to drink. I was homeless and you gave me shelter. I was in prison and you visited me, I was naked and you clothed me. "*

"When did we do all these things?" those on his right hand wondered. He replied, *"Inasmuch as ye have done it unto one of the least of these my brethren, ye have done it unto me "(Matthew 25:40).*

So, said Paul, *"As we have therefore opportunity, let us do good unto all men, especially unto them who are of the household of faith"(Galatians 6:10).* We take care of our own – that is one way we practice our faith – and we let our generosity overflow to those who are not of the faith.

Then there is the matter of the promises God has made for us. How could we take them for granted? And the vision of the new heaven and the new earth seen by John. This is nothing to take for granted.

> *And I saw a new heaven and a new earth: for the first*
> *heaven and the first earth were passed away; and*
> *there was no more sea. And I John saw the holy city,*
> *new Jerusalem, coming down from God out of*
> *heaven, prepared as a bride adorned for her husband.*
> *And I heard a great voice out of heaven saying,*
> *Behold, the tabernacle of God is with men, and he*
> *will dwell with them, and they shall be his people, and*
> *God himself shall be with them, and be their God.*
> *And God shall wipe away all tears from their eyes;*

and there shall be no more death, neither sorrow, nor crying, neither shall there be any more pain: for the former things are passed away (Revelation 21:1-4).

Later, there is this:

And he showed me a pure river of water of life, clear as crystal, proceeding out of the throne of God and of the Lamb. In the midst of the street of it, and on either side of the river, was there the tree of life, which bare twelve manner of fruits, and yielded her fruit every month: and the leaves of the tree were for the healing of the nations. And there shall be no more curse: but the throne of God and of the Lamb shall be in it; and his servants shall serve him: And they shall see his face; and his name shall be in their foreheads (Revelation 22:1-4).

You wouldn't want to take that for granted, would you? *"Behold, I come quickly: blessed is he that keepeth the sayings of the prophecy of this book"* – who practices his faith. Finally, there is this. Something no one in his right mind would ever want to take for granted.

I Jesus have sent mine angel to testify unto you these things in the churches. I am the root and the offspring of David, and the bright and morning star. And the Spirit and the bride say, Come. And let him that heareth say, Come. And let him that is athirst come. And whosoever will, let him take the water of life freely. For I testify unto every man that heareth the words of the prophecy of this book, If any man shall add unto these things, God shall add unto him the plagues that are written in this book: And if any man shall take away from the words of the book of this prophecy, God shall take away his part out of the book of life, and out of the holy city, and from the things which are written in this book. He which testifieth these things saith, Surely I come quickly. Amen. Even so, come, Lord Jesus. The grace of our Lord Jesus Christ be with you all. Amen (Revelation 22:16-21).

---

i. Hebrews 12:25.

ii. Acts 3:1.

iii. See Leviticus 11:1 ff.

21

The God Who Does not Hear

For I was an hungered, and ye gave me no meat:
I was thirsty, and ye gave me no drink:
I was a stranger, and ye took me not in:
naked, and ye clothed me not: sick, and in prison,
and ye visited me not (Matthew 25:42-43 KJV).

How does God work? When he makes a move to answer prayer, what does he actually *do?* We know what he *can* do. You could pray that God would give you something to eat, and when you open your eyes, you could have a steaming bowl of lentil soup and a loaf of fresh baked bread right there on the table. The soup could even have the right amount of black pepper sprinkled across the top. God could do that, but we know all too well that he does not. My question is, since that is not how he does it, how *does* he do it?

Jesus made what some people call "an unconditional promise" in the sermon on the mount. He said, "Ask, and it shall be given you; seek, and ye shall find; knock, and it shall be opened unto you: For every one that asketh receiveth; and he that seeketh findeth; and to him that knocketh it shall be opened" (Matthew 7:7-8).

In context, Jesus is talking about food. "What man is there," Jesus asked, "if his son asks for bread, will give him a stone." So after all, if we human beings, who have a hard time being good, know how to give good things to our children, how much more should our heavenly Father give good things to those who ask him? It is a completely logical and sensible statement. So how come it doesn't seem to work that way?

Jerome Murphy-O'Connor (2004) pointed to the "objective reality" of that statement and how the early Christians might have taken it.[i] I found myself wondering the same thing, because if a woman prays for bread for her starving child, she knows *objectively* whether she got the bread or not.

I have often pondered the implications of answered prayer because I get so many prayer requests, most from people I don't even know. For example, I could get a prayer request from a person who is applying for a given job and wants prayer that he would get the job. I could conceivably get another prayer request from another person applying for the same job, and I would have no idea there was a conflict. How might God answer those two prayers?

O'Connor pointed out something I had overlooked in the passage I just cited. It doesn't stop with the encouraging statement that God will give us good things. It continues with a "therefore." Here is what Jesus said.

> *If ye then, being evil, know how to give good gifts unto your children, how much more shall your Father which is in heaven give good things to them that ask him?* **Therefore** *all things whatsoever ye would that men should do to you, do ye even so to them: for this is the law and the prophets (Matthew 7:11-12).*

How is the "Therefore" clause related to what has gone before? Here is what Jerome Murphy-O'Connor concluded:

> "God uses intermediaries – our fellow men – who in some cases act like genuine Christians and in other instances fail in their duty. For Matthew, this explains why some prayers are answered, while others are not."[ii]

While I am not sure I can endorse all of Murphy-O'Connor's conclusions, I have to acknowledge that God, for his own reasons, decided long ago to use intermediaries. Once, God spoke himself from Mount Sinai, and neither the mountain or the people would ever be the same. Later, he sent his son who spoke to us. Apart from these two profound exceptions, God speaks and acts through intermediaries.

This is what Paul was driving at when he defended himself to the Corinthians. *"Therefore seeing we have this ministry, "*he wrote, *"as we have received mercy, we faint not; But have renounced the hidden things of dishonesty, not walking in craftiness, nor handling the word of God deceitfully; but by manifestation of the truth commending ourselves to every man's conscience in the sight of God"* *(2 Corinthians 4:1-2).*

Consider this. Paul had a choice. He might not have renounced dishonesty, craftiness, and deceit. God knows there are ministers who have *not* done so. And when they don't, it is not God who has failed, but the minister. Paul continues:

> *But if our gospel be hid, it is hid to them that are lost: In whom the god of this world hath blinded the minds of them which believe not, lest the light of the glorious gospel of Christ, who is the image of God, should shine unto them. For we preach not ourselves, but Christ Jesus the Lord; and ourselves your servants for Jesus' sake (vv. 3-5).*

And God also knows that there are ministers who *do* preach themselves. Paul's contrast is deliberate.

> *For God, who commanded the light to shine out of darkness, hath shined in our hearts, to give the light of the knowledge of the glory of God in the face of Jesus Christ. But we have this treasure in earthen vessels, that the excellency of the power may be of God, and not of us (vv. 6-7).*

What a marvelous image that evokes. We hold the treasure of God in our hands, But we ourselves are earthenware pots. It is not the treasure that presents the problem, but the crock in which it is held. So yes, God does indeed work through intermediaries. That is how the Gospel is preached. Jesus said, "All power is given unto *me* in heaven and in earth. Go *you* therefore, and teach all nations" (Matthew 28:18-19).

What is not stated, but is nonetheless true, is that it is possible for us to fail in the task. Paul knew this all too well. *'Though I be free from all men, "* he said, *'I made myself servant unto all, that I might gain the more.*

> *And unto the Jews I became as a Jew, that I might gain the Jews; to them that are under the law, as under the law, that I might gain them that are under the law; To them that are without law, as without law, (being not without law to God, but under the law to Christ,) that I might gain them that are without law. To the weak became I as weak, that I might gain the weak: I am made all things to all men, that I might by all means save some (1 Corinthians 9:18-22).*

And what happens if we don't do our jobs? Implicit in Paul's statement is the fact that he might have done otherwise. He believed that what he did made a difference in the lives of the people he served. Murphy-O'Connor makes the point this way: "For Matthew, the Golden Rule means: 'If you wish others to answer your prayers, then you answer their prayers.'"

Now I don't know whether he is correct in describing what Matthew thinks, but he says something here that deserves serious thought.

> Only now does the absolute character of the promise of Jesus become intelligible: If people ask for what they truly need in a community of love, then the response will certainly be forthcoming. No woman desperate for food for a starving child will be turned away empty-handed if her neighbors are dedicated to meeting the needs of others. Her degree of faith or her moral character is completely irrelevant. Her need and that of her child are paramount.

The God who answers prayers is present within history in the person of Jesus, who after his resurrection continues to be present in the community: "I will be with you all days until the end of the age." God acts through Christ who acts through the community.

When it comes to answering prayers, the members of the believing community are the hands and ears of God. If the community does not listen, God does not hear. The hands that offer bread to the starving are human hands animated by the self-sacrificing love of Christ. If those hands do not reach out, God's will to give is frustrated. [iii]

While it may seem that Murphy-O'Connor is limiting God, I don't think that is the intent at all. In a very real sense, *God limits himself* when he declines to take away our freedom to act or not act. Look at it this way. If a man comes to me to apply for a job, am I free to hire him or to turn down his application? If I don't have that freedom then neither of us it truly free.

I think what he is trying to tell us is that God hasn't gone deaf. Christians have become lazy. We ask God to give us good leadership and then refuse to vote. We know we have poor people in our own community, but we leave the care of them to the State and to God. We think we aren't responsible, the State is. Or God is. We have other things more demanding to do.

We know from endless repetition that faith without works is dead. So we have no excuse for our laziness. And I will add to what is said to this extent. God hasn't gone deaf, but too many Christians have absented themselves from the community of saints.

The work of the Holy Spirit is subtle. It does not normally multiply the loaves and fishes, but it may well suggest to us which side of the boat to fish on. When Jesus told Peter and his friends to drop their net on the other side of the boat, he could just as easily have filled the net where it was. Instead, he suggested they try something different.

For his own reasons God works through human instruments.

Even when he works through the Holy Spirit, where does the Holy Spirit find something to get hold of? Archimedes said that if you gave him a lever long enough, he could move the world. But he would still need a fulcrum and a place to stand.

Where does the Holy Spirit stand and what is its fulcrum? The author of the Book of Hebrews suggests that the assembly of the saints is the lever by which the Spirit works: *"And let us consider one another to provoke unto love and to good works: Not forsaking the assembling of ourselves together, as the manner of some is; but exhorting one another: and so much the more, as ye see the day approaching" (Hebrews 10:24-25).*

So, a brother or a sister comes knocking at our door, hungry and cold. May we stand and bless him saying, "Go in peace, my brother, be warmed and filled," and then close the door in his face? What good have we done him, James wants to know, reminding us that faith, without works, is dead (James 2:14-17).

Surely we would never say to a man, "Don't worry brother. God will take care of you," and then refuse to help, would we? Jesus' most fundamental teaching to his disciples, went to this simple truth. It was even the seal by which others would identify them as disciples of Jesus: "A new commandment I give unto you, That ye love one another; as I have loved you, that ye also love one another. By this shall all men know that ye are my disciples, if ye have love one to another."

So, back to my original question: How does God work? How does he choose to answer prayer? Should it be surprising that we would be the instruments through which these answers flow? Should it be surprising if it turns out that the reason your prayers weren't answered is because you were separated from those whom God would have moved to answer them?

And wouldn't it be a terrible shame if our prayers were not answered because the Christian community was too lazy to do its duty?

---

i. "Why Doesn't God Answer Prayers," Bible Review, April, 2004.

ii. Ibid.

iii. Ibid.

22

Rich toward God

You have planted much, but have harvested little.
You eat, but never have enough. You drink, but never
have your fill. You put on clothes, but are not warm.
You earn wages, only to put them in a purse with holes in it. [i]

I cannot remember a time when the economic picture was good, and I'm over 70 years old. You would think there would have been some good times in 70 years. They tell me 1928 and early 1929 were pretty exciting. But for as long as I can recall (or for as long as I have been paying attention), there has always been something wrong with the economy. We've had inflation, recession, high unemployment, trade deficits, high interest rates, stagflation, an oil shortage, an oil glut, a weak dollar, a strong dollar, an arms race, a steadily rising poverty level, and a great depression, not necessarily in that order.

Now I'm not an economist, but perhaps I can be forgiven for suggesting that there is something a little weird in all this. In case you haven't noticed, try analyzing what they tell you and see if I'm right. No matter what the economy does, there will be no shortage of economists on the morning news with worried faces, gloomy forecasts, and grim predictions of what can happen if this remedy or that cure is not forthcoming. It's almost as if we were surrounded by economic hypochondriacs. Is our economy *really* as bad as the party that's out of power always says it is?

Most of us can sympathize with some ancient Israelites who, according to the prophet, earned wages only to put them into a bag with holes. In their case, there was a reason why things were going wrong. Fifteen years earlier, they had made a start in building the Temple only to cease when intimidated by their neighbors. Since that time, no work had been done on the house of God. Then one day a prophet arrived with a message: "Thus speaketh the Lord of hosts, saying, This people say, The time is not come, the time that the Lord's house should be built" (Haggai 1:2-4).

According to Haggai, the people had left off building God's house, and instead built their own homes, planted crops, and went about their own business. Meanwhile, the Temple of God lay still in ruins. God seems to have taken this neglect quite seriously.

Even in the twentieth century, that scripture has a familiar ring. We know how it feels to work hard for our money and then wonder where it all went. What is the solution to the problem? Well, Haggai didn't leave that question hanging:

> *Thus saith the Lord of hosts; Consider your ways. Go up to the mountain, and bring wood, and build the house; and I will take pleasure in it, and I will be glorified, saith the Lord. Ye looked for much, and, lo, it came to little; and when ye brought it home, I did blow upon it. Why? Saith the Lord of hosts. Because of mine house that is waste, and ye run every man unto his own house (vv. 7-9).*

The lesson behind this is hard to miss. The failure to honor God with your work and your substance can have *economic* consequences. And God being a God who doesn't change, this will be true in any age of man. Jesus, in one of his parables, tells of a certain rich man who had an exceptional harvest. He had so much foodstuff that he had no place to put it. "What can I do with all this," he asked himself. "I know," he said at last. "I will tear down my barns and build bigger barns. And I will say to my soul, 'Soul, thou hast much goods laid up for many years: Take your ease, eat, drink, and be merry.'" He thought he wouldn't have to work again for years. So, what was God's response to this man?

> *You fool, this night your soul shall be required of you: then whose shall these things be, which you have provided? So is he that lays up treasure for himself, and is not rich toward God (Luke 12:16-21).*

But why? What evil had he done? What law had he broken? I don't think this parable is saying that God would kill the man because he didn't bring an offering. But we are all going to die, and of what value is all our wealth then? You can't take it with you, as we are so often reminded.

This parable is important because it is a warning against covetousness, but neither the Greek nor the Hebrew words for "covet" necessarily imply evil. The words may also be translated "greatly desire." For example, Paul encouraged the Corinthians to "covet earnestly the best gifts" (I Corinthians 12:31).

Under what circumstances, then, is coveting a sin? The commandment reads this way: "Thou shalt not covet . . . *anything that is thy neighbors*" (Exodus 20:17). Coveting is only a sin when you desire something unlawful or something that belongs to someone else. But the rich man in this parable had planted his own seed in his own land. He had cultivated it with his own sweat. He had gone into his own field and harvested his own crops. How could he covet what he already owned?

The only way this man could be guilty of covetousness is if God laid prior claim to some portion of his wealth. Jesus plainly teaches in this parable that the man who has enjoyed the bounty of God's good green earth owes a material obligation to God. The existence of an obligation implies a standard. If a man is not free to give little or no offering as he sees fit, he is not free at all. He is *obliged* to be "rich" toward God, but how rich? And, more to the point, Why?

When Israel was ready to enter the Promised Land, God gave them a set of laws and promises which taken together comprised a covenant – a deal. Speaking through Moses, he laid out the foundation of the law and followed it with promises of blessing and warnings of responsibility. He made it clear to them that one result of obedience to the commandments of God was material blessing – even wealth! [ii]

But there is a perversity in human nature. We remember God when times are bad, and we forget God when times are good. It was true of the ancient Israelites and it is still true of modern man. The solemn warning of Moses to the Israelites carries just as much urgency today:

> *Beware that you forget not the Lord your God, in not keeping His commandments . . . lest when you have eaten and are full, and have built goodly houses and have dwelt therein; and when your herds and your flocks multiply and your silver and your gold is multiplied and all that you have is multiplied; then your heart be lifted up and you forget the Lord your God . . . and you say in your heart, My power and the might of my hand has gotten me this wealth. You shall remember the Lord your God: for it is He that gives you power to get wealth (Deuteronomy 8:11-18).*

This passage rings with the echo of Jesus' parable. The rich man in Jesus' parable was judged because he was ignoring the source of his *power* to get wealth – he was denying God. It is required of every man in every age to acknowledge God as the source of his wealth. But what form does this acknowledgment take? Of course we can always get on our knees and thank God for the good things God has given us. But it seems Jesus required some sort of *material* acknowledgment from the rich man. As King Solomon put it, "Honor the Lord with your *substance*, and with the firstfruits of all your increase: so shall your barns be filled with plenty, and your presses shall burst out with new wine" (Proverbs 3:9).

There is, therefore, a clear connection between our generosity toward God and our own economic well being. The rich man had also broken the Tenth Commandment. He had coveted something that belonged to God.

But why does God lay *prior* claim to our substance? Does he need something from us? Is he impoverished, and are we called upon to give sacrificially in order to somehow enrich him? Hardly. God needs nothing from the hand of man. Not only does God own the world and its wealth, but he owns *us* as well. In another Psalm, God says to man:

> *I will take no bullock out of your house nor the goats our of thy folds. For every beast of the forest is mine, and the cattle upon a thousand hills. I know all the fowls of the mountains: and the wild beasts of the field are mine! If I were hungry I would not tell you for the world is mine and the fulness thereof (Psalm 50:9-12).*

By this reckoning everything the rich man had placed in his barn *actually belonged to God.* In that case, he not only had coveted, he was a thief as well. Do we call a man a thief who merely retains what is his own, or is he not a thief when he takes something which belongs to another? Unless or until he had fulfilled his obligation to God, none of this produce was really his. But just what was that obligation?

"Will a man rob God?" Asked another prophet. "Yet you have robbed me. But you say, Wherein have we robbed thee? In *tithes* and *offerings.* You are cursed with a curse: for you have robbed me, even this whole nation" (Malachi 3:8). The Israelites of Malachi's day, and the rich man of Jesus' parable, were robbing God in tithes and offerings. But what were these things called "tithes"? Whatever they were they obviously belonged to God and were His rightful possession.

The exact origins of the law of tithing are obscured by the passage of time, but a systematic study will lead us quickly to a man named Abraham who was a sojourner, a nomad, but also a wealthy, powerful and respected man as well. And he was a man who tithed.

The Book of Genesis records an incident in a war involving the cities of Sodom and Gomorrah. Abraham was a bystander in all this until he learned that the invaders had taken Lot, his nephew, captive along with the two cities. Abraham then armed his trained servants, pursued the kings, defeated them, and brought back all the goods and all the captives.

Upon his return, Abraham was met by a mysterious person named Melchizedek. Being a priest, Melchizedek blessed Abraham and proclaimed that it was the Most High God who delivered his enemies into his hand. Abraham in turn gave Melchizedek tithes, a tenth, of all the booty he had captured (Genesis 14:18).

Who is this Melchizedek? Why would Abraham give him a tenth of all the silver, the gold, the grain, the apparel, the ivory, the precious spices and ointments, and all the rest of the booty of war he had at his disposal? The tithe was given to Melchizedek in acknowledgment that it was indeed the Most High God who had delivered Abraham's enemies into his hand. Abraham saw the tithe as an acknowledgment of God as the source of his power and his victory. It was an outward manifestation of Abraham's faith in God who gave him the victory.

But in a way, it was more than that. All that silver, gold, apparel, and wealth belonged to God. He had rescued it from the hands of thieves and since the former owners had not tithed, Abraham did it for them.

His grandson, Jacob, saw it the same way. After his vision of the heavenly ladder, Jacob made a vow to God (Genesis 28:10 ff.). He promised that if God would be with him and keep him, if God would give him goods and raiment and bring him home in peace, then the Lord would be his God. He continued by saying, "And of all that you shall give me, I will surely give the tenth unto you" (verse 22). The tithe was Jacob's acknowledgment of God as the source of his wealth.

So the law of tithing is clearly of ancient origin and its meaning was clear right from the start. The argument is sometimes made that neither Abraham nor Jacob tithed as a matter of law. We don't know that, because we know so little of the law before Moses. But if you have followed me so far, you will notice that I have said very little about law. The law deals with the *disposition* of the tithe, but has next to nothing to say about the *collection* of the tithe. There was no IRS in God's economy. The tithe was an act of worship, not merely an act of law. So for the moment, let's consider that what Jacob did was an act of worship at his own volition. It was a part of his covenant with God. Listen to what he said.

And Jacob awaked out of his sleep, and he said,
Surely the LORD is in this place; and I knew it not.
And he was afraid, and said, How dreadful is this
place! this is none other but the house of God, and
this is the gate of heaven. And Jacob rose up early in
the morning, and took the stone that he had put for his
pillows, and set it up for a pillar, and poured oil upon
the top of it. And he called the name of that place
Bethel: but the name of that city was called Luz at the
first. And Jacob vowed a vow, saying, If God will be
with me, and will keep me in this way that I go, and
will give me bread to eat, and raiment to put on, So
that I come again to my father's house in peace; then
shall the LORD be my God: And this stone, which I
have set for a pillar, shall be God's house: and of all
that thou shalt give me I will surely give the tenth
unto thee (Genesis 28:16-22).

Here is the question we should ask ourselves as New Covenant Christians: What part of our life do we want to exclude from that covenant? Do you want to exclude your marriage, or is that a part of your deal with Christ? Do you want to exclude your job? You don't want God's help in finding a job and keeping it? Do you want to exclude your children? Surely not in this evil generation. Do you want to exclude your health from the deal? Then why would you want to exclude your finances?

We have already seen in the parable of the rich man that Jesus plainly taught that those who have enjoyed God's blessing are *obliged* to be rich toward God. The existence of an obligation implies the existence of a standard. But what was that standard? Did Jesus teach tithing? The only standard of financial obligation found anywhere in the Bible is the tithe. Jesus himself acknowledged this standard in a confrontation with the Pharisees:

Woe unto you scribes and Pharisees, hypocrites! For
you pay tithes of mint and anise and cumin, and have
omitted the weightier matters of the law, judgment,
mercy, and faith; these ought you to have done, and

> *not to leave the other [paying tithes] undone"*
> *(Matthew 23:23).*

Strangely, there are those who feel they can give attention to "judgment, mercy and faith" while they omit tithing! But Jesus' statement is plain enough: judgment, mercy, faith, *and tithing*, ought to be done.

While the Apostle Paul has no occasion to specifically address tithing in his letters, he does seem to assume it. In writing to the Corinthians, a Gentile church, he is at some pains to establish the right of the ministry to be supported by the membership:

> *If we have sown unto you spiritual things, is it a great*
> *thing if we shall reap your carnal things? If others be*
> *partakers of this power over you, are not we rather?*
> *Nevertheless we have not used this power; but suffer*
> *all things, lest we should hinder the gospel of Christ*
> *(I Corinthians 9:8-12).*

The expression "power over you" is significant. This is not merely an exhortation for a freewill offering, but the assertion of a *right*. If the Corinthians then were under some authority as to how and when and how much they should give to the ministry, what is that authority? If there is a standard of giving, what is that standard? The *only* standard in the Bible is the tenth.

Paul continues his argument: "Do you not know that they which minister about holy things live of the things of the temple? And they which wait at the altar are partakers with the altar? *Even so* hath the Lord ordained that they which preach the gospel should live of the gospel" (vv. 13-14).

The priests in the Temple lived not only of the tithes, but also of many of the offerings that were brought to be presented before God. It is important that Paul asserts the same authority, the same right for the ministry that God gave to the priesthood. In the Book of Hebrews, the author addresses the tithe much more specifically. His subject is not so much tithing as it is the ascendancy of the Melchizedec priesthood over the Levitical priesthood. But the primary illustration of that ascendancy is the tithe. The author first refers to Abraham's encounter with Melchizedek. In so doing, he describes Melchizedek carefully:

> *For this Melchisedec, King of Salem, Priest of the Most High God, who met Abraham returning from the slaughter of the kings, and blessed him; To whom also Abraham gave a tenth part of all [a tithe]; first being by interpretation King of righteousness, and after that also King of Salem, which is, King of peace; Without father, without mother, without descent, having neither beginning of days, nor end of life; but made like unto the Son of God; abideth a priest continually (Hebrews 7:1-3).*

Who could possibly fit this description? Certainly not an angel, because angels are created beings and therefore had a "beginning of days." Melchizedek is no mere mortal, because he has no "end of life." He is, to put it simply, *eternal.* "The Eternal" in the Old Testament is none other than the Creator of the heavens and earth, the "Word" of John 1:1, the giver of the Ten Commandments, *the God of Abraham.* He was also Abraham's friend. He appeared to him repeatedly, shared his thoughts and even a meal with him. It would appear that Abraham was in very regular contact with the person here called Melchizedek. He is the Old Testament manifestation of the one you and I have come to know as Jesus Christ.

"Now consider how great this man was, unto whom even the patriarch Abraham gave a tenth [a tithe] of the spoils." The author is in the process of developing a vitally important concept for the saints, and he begins by observing the greatness of Melchizedek, noting that Abraham – the greatest of the patriarchs – acknowledged that Melchizedek was even greater by paying tribute to him, and *that tribute was the tithe*!

But why a tenth? Why not a ninth or an eleventh? Why aren't the specific terms of the offering listed? Why is any amount given at all? And why does the writer of Hebrews compare it with the "Levitical" tithe? Was Abraham's tithe a random occurrence, or did the tithe have significance – was it already a part of God's law?

171

The writer of Hebrews explains it for us. As we have already pointed out, his subject in this seventh chapter is not the tithe, but the ascendancy of the Melchizedek priesthood. Melchizedek is presented as not only greater than Abraham, but also greater than Levi. "And as I may so say, Levi also, who received tithes, payed tithes in Abraham. For he was yet in the loins of his father, when Malchizedec met him."

The Levitical priesthood was temporary. It was to be superseded by the priesthood of Jesus Christ who is of the "order" of Melchizedek. The subject is the change in the priesthood and the writer acknowledges that "For the priesthood being changed, there is made of necessity a change also of the law." That means that any law, including tithing, had to undergo some change when the priesthood passed from Levi to Christ. Since Jesus Christ received tithes as Melchizedek; since the tithe was due to him from the beginning; and since he gave that tithe to Levi in the first place; he clearly had the right to take it back. The writer of Hebrews is establishing that the priesthood of Jesus Christ has the full right to accept the tithes that had previously been paid to Levi. Neither the priesthood nor tithing were abolished. They were simply transferred back to their original source.

Well, then, how and where is one to pay his tithes, and how are they to be used? There came a time when God set apart a ministry to do His Work. That ministry was composed of the descendants of Levi. When he divided the land of Canaan and gave a portion to all the other tribes, he gave none to Levi – they were to have no *inheritance* in the land. Instead of an inheritance, God gave them the tithe: "And, behold, I have given the children of Levi all the tenth in Israel for an inheritance, for their service which they serve, even the service of the tabernacle of the congregation" (Numbers 18:21).

There are some very important points in this passage. First, the tithe was God's to give. The law recorded here *does not originate the tithe*. The tithe had been long in existence, as we've already seen. Second, there is no reason to assume that, in turning over the tithe to Levi, God relinquished all future claim upon it. We have already seen in the book of Malachi – written in the Levitical period – that the failure to tithe was robbing God, not robbing Levi. Third, the tithe was given to the Levites, *"for their service which they serve."* There is no reason to assume that the Levites would be authorized to continue receiving tithes when they were no longer doing service. The tithe was not given to them for their retirement, but for the work of God. The destruction of the Temple and the scattering of the Levitical priesthood would bring that service to an end. But would it also bring the tithe to an end?

Neither Abraham nor Jacob needed a Temple or a Levitical priesthood in order to see that they must tithe. They, of course, tithed to Melchizedek, but where is Melchizedek today? Who is our High Priest? The writer of Hebrews tells us in the plainest possible terms that Jesus Christ is our High Priest:

> *The Lord sware and will nor repent, Thou art a priest for ever after the order of Melchisedec: By so much was Jesus made a surety of a better testament. And they truly were many priests, because they were not suffered to continue by reason of death: But this man [Jesus] because He continues ever, had an unchangeable priesthood... For the law maketh men high priests which have infirmity; but the word of the oath, which was since the law, maketh the Son, who is consecrated for evermore.*"[iii]

Christ's priesthood, having replaced Levi, has every right to receive tithes. Can the tithe then be used as a means of finance for the church? If the church is carrying out the Work of Jesus Christ; if it is preaching repentance and remission of sins *in his name*; if it is going forth and making disciples of all nations, baptizing people and teaching them to observe all things Jesus commanded his servants; then the answer is *absolutely yes*.

Remember that the tithe was specifically given to Levi for doing God's Work. All Christians should tithe and *they should tithe to the Work of Jesus Christ*.

There are some other lessons to be learned from Malachi's prophecy. For one thing, it is a prophecy for the last days. Right at the very time of Christ's second coming, it is considered "robbing God," to withhold one's tithes.

It's worthwhile to study the whole Book of Malachi to gain a perspective on why the prophet gave his warning on tithing. In Chapter 1, for example, we find a scathing rebuke of those who were dishonoring God even in their offerings. It wasn't that they were not giving. On the contrary, they were offering bread on God's altar, and they were offering animals in sacrifice to him. But they were offering *polluted* bread and *blind* animals. The prophet logically asks, "offer it now to the governor; will he be pleased with you, or accept thy person?" (Malachi 1:8).

Because of their selfishness and their greed, the prophet was moved to say, "And this have ye done again, covering the altar of the Lord with tears, with weeping, and with crying out, insomuch that He regardeth not the offering any more, or receiveth it with good will at your hand."

It should be clear enough that tithing should be done with joy, gratitude, thanksgiving and praise. A person who gives grudgingly or half-heartedly may well find that God will not receive his offering.

Malachi's prophecy is sobering because it speaks of a curse that descended upon an entire nation because of their failure to acknowledge Him as the source of their wealth. The prophet goes on to exhort, *"Bring ye all the tithes into the storehouse, that there may be meat in mine house, and prove me now herewith, saith the Lord of host, if I will not open you the windows of heaven, and pour you out a blessing, that there shall not be room enough to receive it" (Malachi 3:10).*

Stories abound of those who have claimed this promise and have indeed had miraculous blessings descend upon them after they began to tithe. I ran into just such a story some time ago in a most unexpected place. I probably shouldn't have been surprised, but I wasn't expecting a lecture on religion. I was listening to a nationally-known and highly respected real estate investor. Not content with making a lot of money himself, he was determined to share his secrets with others, and was conducting a seminar on real estate investment in the 1980s.

He and several other experts had spent a couple of days running through a series of lectures on money-making techniques in real estate. Finally, toward the end of the seminar, this gentleman stood to give us one more "technique."

He said, "I want to give you a technique, and I hope you understand it. For practical people in the 80s you need techniques that actually work. When I explain this to you, you may not understand it as a technique, but I hope you realize that I used this technique to make my wealth increase and I can prove to you that this technique works by my own business books."

By this time he had everyone's attention. He continued: "I want to read to you out of a book. It doesn't matter who wrote it. I just want you to listen to it. And don't get turned off by it. I'm just trying to tell you what works."

He raised his book and began to read: "Will a man rob God? Yet you have robbed me. But you say, Wherein have we robbed thee? In tithes and offerings . . ."

By now I was sitting bolt upright. I was shocked, but I should have suspected. I had already known that this man felt a transaction was no good if one person won at the expense of another. He had always espoused the Golden Rule in *all* of his techniques. He had carefully followed what he called the "win-win" philosophy. That means he always tried to structure his deals so that both parties to a transaction were winners. So I wasn't totally surprised as he finished reading the scripture and went on to explain how he and his wife had decided to begin tithing and how six days after that decision they had the largest seminar they had ever had in the history of their business.

"Let me tell you that's the best investment I ever made," he said. "I'm a practical person, believe me. Extremely practical. That is the best thing I have ever done for my business . . . I just wanted to let you know where the credit sometimes has to go." Not only did he openly and *verbally* give credit to God for his success, he gave God ten cents of every dollar he earned to back up his words.

There are others, however, who have been disappointed after beginning to tithe, noting no difference or even finding that things have gotten worse! Why would that happen?

Does tithing *guarantee* economic success? No, tithing may remove an economic curse and guarantee God's blessings upon the things you do, but it will not remove the consequences of your own foolish decisions. Tithing will do nothing to change the odds at the gaming tables, nor will it cause the stock market to go up because you bought a few shares of IBM.

175

When you tithe, you display faith, you obey the law of God, and you acknowledge him as the source of every good thing you have. You gain his blessing, but that includes his promise to do what is *ultimately* good for you. That may or may not be sudden wealth. It is enough for you that you trust him.

But there is one more fundamental truth that we must understand: God owes us nothing. Unfortunately, some seem to feel that by the expediency of tithing they have earned something from God. But Paul asks the question, "For who has known the mind of God? Or who has been His counselor? Or who has first given to Him, and it shall be recompensed to him again?" (Romans 11:34-36).

My wife and I began to tithe at a time when tithing was hard. Our income was barely enough to cover our outgo and sometimes it didn't even do that. We really couldn't afford to tithe – or so we thought. But then one day we asked ourselves, "Can we afford *not* to tithe? Why don't we prove God like he said?"

So, without knowing how we could make it, we wrote our first tithe check. A funny thing happened. At the end of the month, we had a few dollars left over! And we made it the next month and the month after that. We had no idea how it worked. But the fact was that ninety percent of our money was now covering what previously had required all of it.

That was more than 50 years ago and it is still working. If you were going into a new business today and you could take on a partner who could control the weather, who could decide where it would rain and where it would not, who knew precisely where all the energy deposits were located, who could gain you access to the best customers, the best sources of supplies, who could help you find the best prices, the best outlets, do you think you could afford to offer him part of the business?

Right now, today, as you read these words, there is nothing to stop you from making God Almighty your partner. When you think about it, can you afford *not* to tithe?

---

i. Haggai 1:6 NIV.

ii. Deuteronomy 7:12-13.

iii. Hebrews 7:21-28.

23

The Organizing Principle

Go to the ant, thou sluggard; consider her ways,
and be wise: Which having no guide, overseer, or ruler,
Provideth her meat in the summer, and gathereth
her food in the harvest (Proverbs 6:6-8).

On the morning of Pentecost, there were 120 disciples
gathered together to celebrate the festival. They had no discernible
organizational structure beyond the twelve apostles plus 108 other
disciples. By sundown, they had baptized 3000 people. As far as we
can tell, this made no great change in the organization of the
fledgling church. It was now twelve apostles and 3108 members –
give or take a few.

The church continued to grow rapidly in the months that
followed, but there is something odd to note. As far as we can tell,
there was no special change in the character of the church. I say this
is odd, because we would expect that many new members to change
things. It would surely require some organizational changes to
manage a group of people like that.

But it didn't. Why didn't it? Why did nothing immediately
change? Some reasons come to mind. We might think the people who
were being baptized had few cultural differences, but that would be
wrong. We know from the events of the day of Pentecost that many
of them didn't even speak the same language. Well then, they were all
Jews, and perhaps had the same religious training? No, they came

from different traditions of Judaism, and in later years, there were some severe disruptions from these factions, but not yet.

Perhaps it was because the moving of the Holy Spirit was much stronger then than now. But is that necessarily true? Was it inevitable that the power of the Holy Spirit would wane?

This new fledgling movement was filled with the Spirit and the excitement of new beginnings. Caught up in the glow, they were together nearly every day. They shared everything they had with one accord. The Temple was still their central meeting place, but they also met from house to house, *"Praising God, and having favour with all the people. And the Lord added to the church daily such as should be saved" (Acts 2:47).*

It is a fascinating picture. Remember that the initial group of people had come for Pentecost from all over the empire. No one wanted to go home, there was so very much to learn. Physical possessions were meaningless to them. They were selling possessions and goods and sharing with strangers. Their primary activities were listening to the apostles as they taught, to prayers at the Temple, and fellowship meals from house to house. They were in a kind of college of the apostles. *They were organizing and memorizing the Gospel.* It was an essential time for what was to follow.

The third chapter of Acts sees Peter healing a crippled man in dramatic fashion. This poor fellow was carried out daily to the gate of the Temple where he could beg from passers by. Peter and John were going up to the Temple to pray at the hour of prayer, and they saw him there. Peter fixed the man with his gaze and said, *"Look at us."* The man responded, expecting alms from them, but Peter said, *"Silver and gold have I none; but such as I have give I thee: In the name of Jesus Christ of Nazareth rise up and walk" (Acts 3:4-6).*

The healing is marvelous, but as a small aside, Peter was flat broke. He didn't even have pocket change. Remember, this was in the period when they all shared whatever they had. In this case, Peter shared a miracle. The crippled man got up and walked.

The fallout from this event was not what one would hope for. Peter was arrested. He was taken to court and asked by what power or in what authority he had done this. Then Peter, "filled with the Holy Spirit," answered them. This was not a premeditated presentation, but a response to the empowerment of the Holy Spirit. It was precisely what Jesus said would happen:

> *And ye shall be brought before governors and kings for my sake, for a testimony against them and the Gentiles. But when they deliver you up, take no thought how or what ye shall speak: for it shall be given you in that same hour what ye shall speak (Matthew 10:18-19).*

This begins to explain why the early movement functioned so well. It had no formal organization. It only became a church, an assembly, on those occasions when they actually assembled. It seems that at this early stage, the organizing principle of the church was the overt, expected and accepted leading of the Holy Spirit.

Having been warned and let go, Peter returned to his own company and reported everything that had happened. What followed was a great prayer that ended thus:

> *And now, Lord, behold their threatenings: and grant unto thy servants, that with all boldness they may speak thy word, by stretching forth thine hand to heal; and that signs and wonders may be done by the name of thy holy child Jesus (Acts 4:30).*

These people were energized, but what happened next must have taken them to a new level. *"And when they had prayed, the place was shaken where they were assembled together; and they were all filled with the Holy Ghost, and they spake the word of God with boldness" (Acts 4:31).*

The organizing principle of the early Christian movement was the leading and power of the Holy Spirit. What follows in Acts is relevant to that.

> *And the multitude of them that believed were of one heart and of one soul: neither said any of them that ought of the things which he possessed was his own; but they had all things common. And with great power gave the apostles witness of the resurrection of the*

*Lord Jesus: and great grace was upon them all.
Neither was there any among them that lacked: for as
many as were possessors of lands or houses sold
them, and brought the prices of the things that were
sold, And laid them down at the apostles' feet: and
distribution was made unto every man according as
he had need (vv. 32-35)*

It is a remarkable example of unselfishness, and there was
something else going on that we only learn about later. A kind of
ministry had developed to take care of the needs of the widows in the
community of disciples. (There were as many as 8,000 Christians by
this time, and their needs varied.) Yet we know nothing about how
this ministry came into being.

Apparently they were what is today called, "Self-organizing
ministry teams." Someone sees a need, talks to others about it, and
sets out to meet that need without having to be told to do it. It is
based on a principle from the book of Proverbs.

*Go to the ant, thou sluggard; consider her ways, and
be wise: Which having no guide, overseer, or ruler,
Provideth her meat in the summer, and gathereth her
food in the harvest (Proverbs 6:6-8).*

In other words, you don't have to be told everything to do.
You can see a need and you do something about it. You don't have to
be told, and you don't have to ask for permission. I think we can
safely assume that the Holy Spirit led some kind souls to put together
a ministry to provide food to needy widows. Mind you, this was all
happening with no *apparent* organizational structure. But things were
already beginning to change:

*But a certain man named Ananias, with Sapphira his
wife, sold a possession, And kept back part of the
price, his wife also being privy to it, and brought a
certain part, and laid it, at the apostles' feet. But
Peter said, Ananias, why hath Satan filled thine heart
to lie to the Holy Ghost, and to keep back part of the*

price of the land? Whiles it remained, was it not thine own? and after it was sold, was it not in thine own power? why hast thou conceived this thing in thine heart? thou hast not lied unto men, but unto God (Acts 5:1-4).

Note well that Peter said Ananias had lied *to the Holy Spirit.* It was not a church policy or rule that required him to do this. It was the Holy Spirit that was moving men and women to devote themselves to this or that ministry, not a recognized organizational structure. I will repeat this for emphasis: *The leadership of the Holy Spirit was the organizing principle of the early church.*

But now there is a fly in the ointment. Not only do we have the tragic example of Ananias, who was apparently trying to curry favor with the apostles by his false gift, but the entire structure of the care of the poor was beginning to break down.

And in those days, when the number of the disciples was multiplied, there arose a murmuring of the Grecians against the Hebrews, because their widows were neglected in the daily ministration (Acts 6:1).

So what had happened? It was a long standing custom among the Jews to engage in charitable works, and some of them had got together and started a daily ministration to widows. The problem was that there was some lack of symmetry in the way the ministry was being carried on.

The result of this was the very first example of organized or structured ministry in the early church. The first seven deacons were appointed. But a question must be addressed. If everyone had been doing his duty and following the lead of the Holy Spirit, would this have been necessary? Possibly not. It may well be that organization was required because some people were not doing their duty.

That said, there is nothing wrong with organization, but it is not without its cost. An organization uses valuable energy that might have been better spent elsewhere. Why? Because someone has to stop working to organize the work of others.

It can hardly be doubted that the church lost some momentum

from its earliest days. Why was this happening? Was the Holy Spirit becoming less effective? Was God slowly removing the Holy Spirit, or was something else going on?

There is a hint of what might have been wrong in Jesus' parable of the sower and the seed. In this parable, Jesus compares people to different kinds of soil in which seeds are planted. Apart from the good soil that bears fruit, there were three other kinds that did not. It is the third that seems relevant here: *"He also that received seed among the thorns is he that heareth the word; and the care of this world, and the deceitfulness of riches, choke the word, and he becometh unfruitful" (Matthew 13:18-22).*

It isn't credible that God was progressively withholding the Spirit from his people. It is far more likely that life began to intervene. The care of the world, doing a job, feeding the family, fighting off adversity, became a distraction from the business of God. This principle is nowhere more clear than in the letter to the church at Laodicea:

> *And unto the angel of the church of the Laodiceans write; These things saith the Amen, the faithful and true witness, the beginning of the creation of God; I know thy works, that thou art neither cold nor hot: I would thou wert cold or hot. So then because thou art lukewarm, and neither cold nor hot, I will spue thee out of my mouth. Because thou sayest, I am rich, and increased with goods, and have need of nothing; and knowest not that thou art wretched, and miserable, and poor, and blind, and naked (Revelation 3:14-22).*

There can be no doubt what he is talking about here. These are a people who are rich in this world's goods. Physically, they have money. Spiritually, they are bankrupt. The letter goes on to say, *"I counsel thee to buy of me gold tried in the fire, that thou mayest be rich; and white raiment, that thou mayest be clothed, and that the shame of thy nakedness do not appear; and anoint thine eyes with eyesalve, that thou mayest see."*

The early church thrived on persecution, but foundered in prosperity. This is a warning. If the only way God can keep us dependent on His Spirit is by means of persecution, then persecution it will be.

We can't be certain what happened to the first disciples, but perhaps we ought to stop and ask what has happened to us. We don't have to guess about that. We live in the wealthiest nation in the world has ever seen. Most of our *poor* people own a car and have a television and a DVD player. Probably a third of them own their own home and sleep in air conditioned comfort at night. Our poor people are rich compared to most societies around the world. We have become a people preoccupied with *things*, with possessions, with entertainment. Where does it lead?

> *My people are destroyed for lack of knowledge: because thou hast rejected knowledge, I will also reject thee, that thou shalt be no priest to me: seeing thou hast forgotten the law of thy God, I will also forget thy children; therefore will I change their glory into shame (Hosea 4:6-7).*

There is an inescapable connection between wealth, physical comfort, and the loss of contact with God. To one of the early churches, the Lord wrote:

> *Unto the angel of the church of Ephesus write; These things saith he that holdeth the seven stars in his right hand, who walketh in the midst of the seven golden candlesticks; I know thy works, and thy labour, and thy patience, and how thou canst not bear them which are evil: and thou hast tried them which say they are apostles, and are not, and hast found them liars: And hast borne, and hast patience, and for my name's sake hast laboured, and hast not fainted. Nevertheless I have somewhat against thee, because thou hast left thy first love. Remember therefore from whence thou art fallen, and repent, and do the first works; or else I will come unto thee quickly, and will remove thy candlestick out of his place, except thou repent (Revelation 2:1-5).*

I am not calling on the church to sell everything they have and give it to the poor. But I am calling on us as individuals to look for the leading of the Holy Spirit in our lives. The people of the early church at least thought about that. Borrowing from a song, the Holy Spirit was "the wind beneath their wings," the wind of God in their lives. They thought in terms of being filled with the Holy Spirit. The Holy Spirit spoke to them, commissioned them, gave them tasks and sent them out to do them. The Spirit forbade them from going in the wrong direction and gave and withheld permission. The Spirit bore witness through many people. The Holy Sprit appointed men to offices and responsibility. It can be fairly said that the work of the early church was organized and directed by the Holy Spirit.

How can we expect the Holy Spirit to be the organizing principle in our lives and our church when we don't even think about it? And don't talk about it? And don't *credit* it for the things that are done? We may even think we don't need it. After all, we have self-esteem.

Paul warned the Thessalonians, *"Do not put out the Spirit's fire" (1 Thessalonians 5:19 NIV)*. It seems entirely possible to organize the Spirit right out of our midst. Our organized effort conceivably could make no room for the Spirit; it could even get in the way. The leadership of the Spirit could even be an intrusion on our organization.

At the personal level, we might consider the organizing principle of our spiritual life. Our organizational skills, our leadership, our self-esteem are simply not enough. It is the organization given by the all seeing Holy Spirit that makes all the difference.

24

The God Who Lives with Us

*Let not your heart be troubled: ye believe in God, believe also in
me. In my Father's house are many mansions: if it were not so,
I would have told you. I go to prepare a place for you.
And if I go and prepare a place for you, I will come again,
and receive you unto myself; that where I am,
there ye may be also (John 14:1-3).*

We dare not let this promise get away from us in all the
technicalities of dogma. What Jesus does here is introduce the theme
of the entire last evening of Jesus with his disciples. It isn't really
mansions he is talking about. It isn't offices. It isn't rooms. It isn't so
much a question of here on earth or there in heaven. It is a question of
being together.

The root behind the Greek word for "mansion" is the verb "to
abide." I don't want to bore you with Greek, but this is a lot like
"abode" and "abide," a noun and a verb from the same root. The only
reason this is important is that Jesus is making a play on words to
develop his theme. The words are *meno* and *mone*, and they are
driven home in the discourse.

Notice the point of the "mansion" Jesus is preparing: *"that
where I am, there ye may be also."* Jesus immediately continues with
theme and the word play: *"If ye love me, keep my commandments.
And I will pray the Father, and he shall give you another Comforter,
that he may abide with you for ever"* (John 14:15-16). First, we had

the noun, now we have the verb, "In my Father's house, there are many *abodes*, that we may *abide* with you forever."

When Jesus adds the idea of the Comforter, the Counselor, he identifies it as: "The Spirit of truth; whom the world cannot receive, because it seeth him not, neither knoweth him: but ye know him; for he *dwelleth* with you, and shall be in you." I suppose in the interest of variety, the translators change the rendering so that Jesus speaks of mansions, and abiding and dwelling. Jesus seems to have more interest in drumming the point home. The Holy Spirit *abides* with us.

> *I will not leave you comfortless: I will come to you.*
> *Yet a little while, and the world seeth me no more; but*
> *ye see me: because I live, ye shall live also. At that*
> *day ye shall know that I am in my Father, and ye in*
> *me, and I in you. He that hath my commandments,*
> *and keepeth them, he it is that loveth me: and he that*
> *loveth me shall be loved of my Father, and I will love*
> *him, and will manifest myself to him (John 14:18-21).*

Later, a disciple asks how Jesus would show himself to the disciples and not to the world. Jesus answered, "If a man love me, he will keep my words: and my Father will love him, and we will come unto him, and make our *abode* with him" (v. 23). Here the Greek word for "abode" is precisely the same as "mansions" in verse two.

This is Jesus' theme. It is about being together, living together, sharing our digs. My Father will love him, said Jesus, and we will come and *move in.* So when you build a fire in the fireplace, and hold a cup of hot chocolate between your hands while you warm your feet and stare into the fire, you are not alone. Someone is there with you. When you backpack up the mountains and make your camp with a view to dazzle the eyes, you are not alone. Someone is there with you. You may be in a canoe, easing down a river, watching for wildlife. You are not alone.

Jesus continued to talk as they made their way across the brook Kidron, and the theme of his conversation continues to emerge.

> *I am the true vine, and my Father is the husbandman.*
> *Every branch in me that beareth not fruit he taketh*

*away: and every branch that beareth fruit, he purgeth
it, that it may bring forth more fruit. Now ye are clean
through the word which I have spoken unto you.*

*Abide in me, and I in you. As the branch cannot bear
fruit of itself, except it abide in the vine; no more can
ye, except ye abide in me. I am the vine, ye are the
branches: He that abideth in me, and I in him, the
same bringeth forth much fruit: for without me ye can
do nothing. If a man abide not in me, he is cast forth
as a branch, and is withered; and men gather them,
and cast them into the fire, and they are burned. If ye
abide in me, and my words abide in you, ye shall ask
what ye will, and it shall be done unto you. Herein is
my Father glorified, that ye bear much fruit; so shall
ye be my disciples. As the Father hath loved me, so
have I loved you: continue ye in my love. If ye keep
my commandments, ye shall abide in my love; even as
I have kept my Father's commandments, and abide in
his love" (John 15:1-10).*

Nine times in this short passage we encounter the word
"abide" but it is more than that. It is what the whole section is about.
And it doesn't stop there. Unaccountably, every important translation
misses this in verse 11: "These things have I spoken unto you, that
my joy might remain in you, and that your joy might be full." The
word rendered "remain" is *mone*, "abide." I wouldn't think this was
important except that Jesus is driving this point home in his own way.
Even later, he tells his disciples that he has appointed them to go out
and bear fruit, "and that your fruit should *abide*."

Then Jesus warns his disciples about the hatred that is headed
their way: "If the world hated you, ye know that it hated me before it
hated you" (v. 17). It may not seem obvious, but the reason they
would hate Jesus' disciples is because they hated God. They hated the
disciples of Jesus because the Father and Son lived with them.

There is an awful irony in this, because the Jews would also
suffer terrible, implacable hatred down through history. And the
reason may not be apparent to most people. The roots of anti-

semitism are the same as Christian persecution by the Jews. The hatred of God.

The use of the word "abide" passes, but the theme goes on. "I tell you the truth," said Jesus, "It is expedient for you that I go away: for if I go not away, the Comforter will not come unto you; but if I depart, I will send him unto you" (John 16:7).

The "Comforter" is a new idea. The New International Version calls it the "Counselor." In the Greek it is *Parakletos*, a combined form of *para* and *kletos*. We are familiar with para from words like paralegal and paramedic. It means "beside." *Kletos* comes from the verb *kaleo*, to call, and carries the sense of called, invited or appointed.

So, the comforter is the one "appointed alongside." It is, of course, the Holy Spirit, our guide, our counselor, our comforter. It is also the *abiding* presence of Father and Son. The Counselor has duties to perform:

> *And when he is come, he will reprove the world of sin, and of righteousness, and of judgment: Of sin, because they believe not on me; Of righteousness, because I go to my Father, and ye see me no more; Of judgment, because the prince of this world is judged* (John 16:8-11).

There is a small discontinuity here. The Counselor comes to us, but reproves the world. I think what Jesus is saying is that he will reprove the world to us. You may be watching a movie, and the Counselor will tell you that it is trash. The Counselor may ask you why on earth you have brought him to see this. Jesus went on to say:

> *I have yet many things to say unto you, but ye cannot bear them now. Howbeit when he, the Spirit of truth, is come, he will guide you into all truth: for he shall not speak of himself; but whatsoever he shall hear, that shall he speak: and he will show you things to come (vv. 12-13).*

Like the family counselor, the Holy Spirit does not do its own thing. It gets instructions and conveys them to us. And there is a passage in Matthew that bears on this function.

> *And ye shall be brought before governors and kings for my sake, for a testimony against them and the Gentiles. But when they deliver you up, take no thought how or what ye shall speak: for it shall be given you in that same hour what ye shall speak. For it is not ye that speak, but the Spirit of your Father which speaketh in you (Matthew 10:18-20).*

This is where the Counselor comes into the picture in a crucial way. When you get dragged into court, you need an advocate, legal counsel, someone to speak for you. You have it. And you clam up until your "lawyer" tells you what to say. Having said this, Jesus went on:

> *The disciple is not above his master, nor the servant above his lord. It is enough for the disciple that he be as his master, and the servant as his lord. If they have called the master of the house Beelzebub, how much more shall they call them of his household?* (v. 25).

After all, when Father and Son have moved in, we are the household of God.

There is a marvelous old hymn, one we often sing without thinking twice about the words. Henry F. Lyte wrote the song in 1847 while he was dying of tuberculosis. He finished it the day he gave his farewell sermon in the parish he served so many years. The next day, he left for Italy to regain his health. He didn't make it, though – he died in France, three weeks later. Here is an excerpt from his farewell sermon:

> O brethren, I stand here among you today, as alive from the dead, if I may hope to impress it upon you, and induce you to prepare for that solemn hour which must come to all, by a timely acquaintance with the death of Christ.

The bells of his church at All Saints in Lower Brixham, Devonshire, have rung out the words of his hymn ever since. The hymn was sung at the wedding of King George VI of Britain, and at the wedding of his daughter, the future Queen Elizabeth II. The tune is "Eventide."

Abide with me; fast falls the eventide;
The darkness deepens; Lord with me abide.
When other helpers fail and comforts flee,
Help of the helpless, O abide with me.

Swift to its close ebbs out life's little day;
Earth's joys grow dim; its glories pass away;
Change and decay in all around I see;
O Thou who changest not, abide with me.

Not a brief glance I beg, a passing word;
But as Thou dwell'st with Thy disciples, Lord,
Familiar, condescending, patient, free.
Come not to sojourn, but abide with me.

Come not in terrors, as the King of kings,
But kind and good, with healing in Thy wings,
Tears for all woes, a heart for every plea—
Come, Friend of sinners, and thus bide with me.

Thou on my head in early youth didst smile;
And, though rebellious and perverse meanwhile,
Thou hast not left me, oft as I left Thee,
On to the close, O Lord, abide with me.

I need Thy presence every passing hour.
What but Thy grace can foil the tempter's power?
Who, like Thyself, my guide and stay can be?
Through cloud and sunshine, Lord, abide with me.

I fear no foe, with Thee at hand to bless;
Ills have no weight, and tears no bitterness.
Where is death's sting? Where, grave, thy victory?
I triumph still, if Thou abide with me.

Chances are you have sung this hymn without fully considering the words. We take it for granted, but it is really a bit frightening to pray this prayer. It may be comforting when you are dying, but at other times, it is daunting. Do I really want God looking over my shoulder as I do this thing? Do I want him to *abide* with me? Really? Right now?

25

Worship in Truth

All the earth bows down to you;
they sing praise to you, they sing praise to your name.
Come and see what God has done,
how awesome his works in man's behalf! [i]

The worship of God is not as easy as you might think. It is easy enough to *pretend* to worship. All the forms are well known. Raised hands, bowed head, bent knees. The jargon of praise is easily learned. Songs are easy enough if you can carry a tune. But something should tell us that it is not that easy. Not really. Not in truth.

Jesus met a woman at a well in Samaria. She said to him:

Sir, I perceive that thou art a prophet. Our fathers worshipped in this mountain; and ye say, that in Jerusalem is the place where men ought to worship. Woman, believe me," Jesus said, *"the hour cometh, when ye shall neither in this mountain, nor yet at Jerusalem, worship the Father. . .But the hour cometh, and now is, when the true worshippers shall worship the Father in spirit and in truth: for the Father seeketh such to worship him. God is a Spirit: and they that worship him must worship him in spirit and in truth" (John 4:19-24).*

Jesus makes it clear enough. Worship is not a matter of place, but of spirit. But what did he mean by that?

"Come, let us sing for joy to the LORD;" cried the psalmist, *"let us shout aloud to the Rock of our salvation" (Psalms 95:1 NIV).* That would certainly be spirited. I have been in a service where the leader tried to lead a cheer for Jesus. We were called upon to shout aloud in praise of God. We did, but there was to me something false about it. It was not at all like the shout that goes up when a football team scores. It wasn't even as good as "Give me an E," with cheerleaders leading us at the game.

The Psalm goes on to speak of bowing down and kneeling before God. Is it an expression of great reverence or is it mere religious form? We have to face the fact that our hearts *have* been hardened to such things, but we also have to realize that the cure is not pretense.

In John's apocalyptic vision, he witnessed a spontaneous act of worship on the part of 24 enigmatic figures. He was ushered through an open door in heaven and found himself in the throne room of God himself. In the center, there was a throne, and the one who sat on the throne glowed with shades of green and red. There was something like a green iris radiating from the throne (Revelation 4:1-3).

In a circle around the throne, there were 24 thrones and seated on them were 24 elders, each dressed in white and each wearing a crown of gold. These are figures of great mystery. They are righteous, because they are dressed all in white. They are powerful, because they sit on thrones and wear crowns. But read what happens as God appears on the throne accompanied by peals of thunder and flashes of lightning, and the heralds announce him: *"Holy, holy, holy is the Lord God Almighty, who was, and is, and is to come."*

> *The twenty-four elders fall down before him who sits*
> *on the throne, and worship him who lives for ever and*
> *ever. They lay their crowns before the throne and say:*
> *"You are worthy, our Lord and God, to receive glory*
> *and honor and power, for you created all things, and*

by your will they were created and have their being
(Revelation 4:10-11).

This is real worship, not mere form. They are privileged to see the one sitting on the throne in the midst. They know him and they know what he has done. This worship comes from knowing, from experience, from, well, from truth.

The worship also comes from fear. God is all good, but he is not soft or safe. He is downright dangerous. There is no pretense in this place.

When we read or sing a Psalm, we may not appreciate the spring from which it comes. Take the 66th Psalm, for instance.

Shout with joy to God, all the earth! Sing the glory of
his name; make his praise glorious! Say to God,
"How awesome are your deeds! So great is your
power that your enemies cringe before you.

Now you may think some Jewish scribe sat down and wrote that Psalm one day to have a Psalm for a worship service. But that is not the origin of this Psalm. It was sung first on the bank of the Red Sea. Moses and all Israel had just walked dry shod across the bottom with water like a wall on both sides. Pharaoh's chariots were thundering in pursuit. And then, when the last Israelite was clear of the water and all of Pharaoh's chariots were still down there, the walls of water collapsed and drowned them all.

Now, can you imagine a shout from the tens of thousands lining the banks of the sea? The explosion of pent up fear, the joy of knowing they can live free? No divine cheerleader is required. Hear in this Psalm the intense satisfaction and joy of a people who have been set free after a time of terrible bondage:

All the earth bows down to you; they sing praise to
you, they sing praise to your name. Come and see
what God has done, how awesome his works in man's
behalf! He turned the sea into dry land, they passed
through the waters on foot—come, let us rejoice in
him. He rules forever by his power, his eyes watch the

nations-- let not the rebellious rise up against him.
Praise our God, O peoples, let the sound of his praise
be heard; he has preserved our lives and kept our feet
from slipping. For you, O God, tested us; you refined
us like silver. You brought us into prison and laid
burdens on our backs. You let men ride over our
heads; we went through fire and water, but you
brought us to a place of abundance (Psalm 66:4-12).

This is what it means to worship in spirit and in truth. When you are singing hymns next time ask yourself this about the song you are singing? Did this get written because the man wanted to write a song this week, or did it arise from a very real worship of God, a life experience so deep that he could not help but write it? Is it a song that arose from the heart like the shout when the waters covered Pharaoh's army? Or is it a cry from the heart of one wounded in spirit, yet trusting God all the time?

I know you have heard of the Chicago fire in 1871. One-hundred-thousand people lost their homes. It was a mercy that only 300 died. There was a lawyer in Chicago who had invested heavily in real estate that burned in the fire. Yet, for the next two years, he worked hard helping people who had lost everything to the fire. His only son died about the same time, but his wife and four daughters were with him. I doubt that you would recognize his name.

When things started getting back to normal, he decided to go to England with his wife and four daughters. He himself was delayed, but he sent his wife and daughters on ahead. He would catch them in England. The daughters never made it. Their ship was involved in a collision off Newfoundland and went down quickly. His wife clung to a piece of flotsam, and was rescued. His daughters, Maggie, Tanetta, Annie and Bessie, were lost at sea. He learned about it with a telegram from his wife.

The lawyer caught the next ship to be with his wife. No one knows exactly when he wrote his hymn, but in those days of sorrow and grief he wrote one of the greatest hymns of all time. His name you may not know and probably won't remember. Horatio Gates Spafford. The hymn, you probably do know *"It Is Well with My Soul."* You can tell when you sing it that it is *worship in truth.* But the story tells you why it is in truth.

When peace like a river, attendeth my way;
When sorrows like sea billows roll;
Whatever my lot, thou hast taught me to say,
It is well, it is well with my soul.

It is well, with my soul. It is well, it is well, with my soul.

Though Satan should buffet, though trials should come,
Let this blest assurance control,
That Christ hath regarded my helpless estate,
And hath shed His own blood for my soul.

It is well, with my soul. It is well, it is well, with my soul.

And, Lord, haste the day when our faith shall be sight
The clouds be rolled back as a scroll,
The trumpet shall sound, and the Lord shall descend;
Even so, it is well with my soul.

It is well, with my soul. It is well, it is well, with my soul.

His name is worth remembering: Horatio Gates Spafford. Having heard that story, and singing that hymn, one begins to wonder what lies behind the great old Psalms that are sung so often and for which so many tunes have been written. The tune "Old 100th" is for the 100th Psalm, but a lot of other tunes are written for it as well.

Make a joyful noise unto the LORD, all ye lands.
Serve the LORD with gladness:
come before his presence with singing.
Know ye that the LORD he is God:
it is he that hath made us, and not we ourselves;
we are his people, and the sheep of his pasture.
Enter into his gates with thanksgiving, and into his
courts with praise:

be thankful unto him, and bless his name.
For the LORD is good; his mercy is everlasting;
and his truth endureth to all generations (Psalm 100).

I don't know what touched W. B. Stevens to write his song,
but I can remember it from my childhood.

Tempted and tried will oft' me to wonder
Why it should be thus all the day long;
While there are others living about us,
Never molested, though in the wrong.

Farther along we'll know more about it.
Farther along we'll understand why;
Cheer up my brother live in the sunshine
We'll understand it all by and by.

When death has come and taken our loved ones
Leaving our homes so lonely and drear;
Then do we wonder how others prosper
Living so wicked year after year.

Farther along we'll know more about it.
Farther along we'll understand why;
Cheer up my brother live in the sunshine
We'll understand it all by and by.

Often I wonder why I must journey
Over a road so rugged and steep;
While there are others living in comfort,
While with the lost I labor and weep.

Faithful 'til death, said our loving Master,
A few more days labor and wait;
Toils of the road will then be as nothing,
As we sweep through the beautiful gates.

Farther along we'll know more about it.
Farther along we'll understand why;
Cheer up my brother live in the sunshine
We'll understand it all by and by.

It is a song Job could have written. Or one of the Psalmists. Maybe you can begin to see what I meant when I said that the worship of God is not as easy as one might think. Sometimes it involves no small amount of pain, grief and loss. But the deepest and truest worship of God comes from that kind of pain. One fellow wrote that he didn't like the Psalms. There was too much anger, too much revenge, too much blood. I understand that, and yet the anger in the Psalms is real. It is a cry of the heart that may not reflect the *final* attitude of the Psalmist, but the worship is real. And it is truth. There is no point in lying or pretending with God. He knows. "O LORD, rebuke me not in thine anger," cried the Psalmist, "neither chasten me in thy hot displeasure" (Psalm 6:1). The man who wrote this Psalm was in deep trouble. He was in pain. He was sick, and his enemies were winning. In his deepest pain and grief, he cries out to God for relief. This kind of worship is simply not possible when all is going well.

And there comes a point in a man's life when he gives up on this world. All hope in this life is gone. There is nothing left for him here. When you get to that place, what does worship entail?

Here's what Carl Blackmore sang:

Some glorious morning sorrow will cease.
Some glorious morning all will be peace;
Heartaches all ended, school-days all done,
Heaven will open, Jesus will come.

Some golden daybreak Jesus will come;
Some golden daybreak, battles all won,
He'll shout the vict'ry, break through the blue,
Some golden daybreak, for me, for you.

—*Carl A. Blackmore*

The deepest and most profound worship of God seems to arise out of the dark night of a man's soul. It can arise out of a fear of God that is entirely justified.

Two sons of Aaron foolishly approached the Tabernacle of God in a way that had not been prescribed. They were like men who go into a high radiation area with no protective clothing. They were burned to a crisp. Aaron and his other sons, being priests, were not even allowed to mourn. Moses explained the fear of the Lord to them instead (Leviticus 10:1-3). Much later, Paul would write:

> *See that ye refuse not him that speaketh. For if they escaped not who refused him that spake on earth, much more shall not we escape, if we turn away from him that speaketh from heaven: Whose voice then shook the earth: but now he hath promised, saying, Yet once more I shake not the earth only, but also heaven. And this word, Yet once more, signifieth the removing of those things that are shaken, as of things that are made, that those things which cannot be shaken may remain. Wherefore we receiving a kingdom which cannot be moved, let us have grace, whereby we may serve God acceptably with reverence and godly fear: For our God is a consuming fire"* (Hebrews 12:25-29).

Remember that when you worship. Leave off all pretense. Our God is compassionate, loving, merciful, *and dangerous*. He is a consuming fire.

---

i. *Psalm 66:4 -5 NIV.*

26

The Judge

"The Lord knoweth how to deliver the godly out of temptations, and to reserve the unjust unto the day of judgment to be punished" (2 Peter 2:9).

We know so little about God, and what we do know is so often confused by theologies that long ago took us down the wrong path. We may even feel that we have taken a wrong turn, but have no idea where it was.

The chances are that we made the same mistake with God that we often make in our human relationships. We fall in love with one attribute of the object of our affection and hope against hope that the things we don't like will go away. We learn, often painfully, that people's uncomfortable traits don't get better over time.

Real friendships and real loves must take the loved one as a whole. People who marry in the hope that their mate will get better are playing a fool's game, but no less foolish than those who remake God in their own image, picking this attribute while ignoring another. We are happy to know that God is loving, merciful, compassionate, caring. We may not be so happy to think on another attribute. God is *just*.

"Just" is a small word with big consequences. The man who was a friend of God called him *"The Judge of all the earth" (Genesis 18:25)*. Any theology that omits God's role as Judge is seriously flawed and misleading, and it is precisely here that so many Christian thinkers go wrong. And they should know better. One reason they don't is because too many give short shrift to the Old Testament.

Jewish thinkers, whatever mistakes we may think they have made, have not forgotten that God is a Judge. Their annual holidays all lead them to think about what the days mean and how they relate to what God is doing. And in the autumn days of Rosh Hashana and Yom Kippur, their thoughts turn to a time of final judgment.

Jewish traditions are not the norm for Christians, but they have been thinking about these issues for a very long time, and must not be lightly dismissed. The days between the Jewish New Year and Yom Kippur are called "The days of awe," or the days of repentance. Here is what one Jewish source says about this.

> One of the ongoing themes of the Days of Awe is the concept that G-d has "books" that he writes our names in, writing down who will live and who will die, who will have a good life and who will have a bad life, for the next year. These books are written in on Rosh Hashanah, but our actions during the Days of Awe can alter G-d's decree. The actions that change the decree are "teshuvah, tefilah and tzedakah," repentance, prayer, good deeds (usually, charity). These "books" are sealed on Yom Kippur. This concept of writing in books is the source of the common greeting during this time is "May you be inscribed and sealed for a good year."[i]

Christian doctrine also includes a "Book of Life," in which names are written. But some Christians are conflicted by a doctrine of predestination which holds that what is to happen in our lives is written, and cannot be changed. The Jews acknowledge that it is written, but also that it can be changed by repentance and a changed life.

A doctrine of *eternal* judgment is found in the most basic list of Christian doctrine.

> *Therefore leaving the principles of the doctrine of*
> *Christ, let us go on unto perfection; not laying again*
> *the foundation of repentance from dead works, and of*
> *faith toward God, Of the doctrine of baptisms, and of*
> *laying on of hands, and of resurrection of the dead,*
> *and of eternal judgment. And this will we do, if God*
> *permit (Hebrews 6:1-3).*

When you think about it, "Eternal Judgment" is an odd expression, but the final judgment of God is for eternity. The expression "final judgment" has a grim sound to it, and yet, we should know that there has to be something like that, some tying up of loose ends, closing of all books, ending the age and perhaps starting anew. Whatever the case, it is in the list of the most basic of doctrines for the Christian faith.

Those Christians who observe the Feast of Trumpets, the day the Jews call "Rosh Hashana," may have a better grasp of the final judgment of God. After all, we believe in a "Book of Life," and we believe that Christ will return at the "last trumpet." What we sometimes forget is that Christ returns for judgment.

We know from the New Testament that God is always judging us, day by day. "*For the time is come,*" said Peter, "*that judgment must begin at the house of God: and if it first begin at us, what shall the end be of them that obey not the gospel of God?*" (1 Peter 4:17).

So there is a temporal judgment as well as a *final* judgment, a day that Jude calls "the judgment of the great day," a time when even the fallen angels will be finally judged: "*The angels which kept not their first estate, but left their own habitation, he hath reserved in everlasting chains under darkness unto the judgment of the great day*" (Jude 1:6).

So there is a judgment day, at least for the fallen angels. What about us mortals? Is there a day when we too must finally be judged? The author of Hebrews says in the clearest of terms that there is a time of judgment for sinners:

> *For if we sin wilfully after that we have received the*
> *knowledge of the truth, there remaineth no more*
> *sacrifice for sins, But a certain fearful looking for of*

judgment and fiery indignation, which shall devour
the adversaries (Hebrews 10:26-27).

The Apostle John had a vision of what that great day of final judgment would be like. Late in the book of Revelation, and after he has seen in vision the resurrection of the saints, which he calls "the first resurrection," he sees a great white throne and the Judge of all sitting there. In this second resurrection, he saw:

the dead, small and great, stand before God; and the
books were opened: and another book was opened,
which is the book of life: and the dead were judged
out of those things which were written in the books,
according to their works. And the sea gave up the
dead which were in it; and death and hell delivered
up the dead which were in them: and they were
judged every man according to their works. And
death and hell were cast into the lake of fire. This is
the second death. And whosoever was not found
written in the book of life was cast into the lake of
fire" (Revelation 20:11-15).

This lake of fire sounds rather final, but then the idea of a final judgment is all through the New Testament. Peter has a long section in his second letter that speaks of it in some detail. [ii]
He begins by speaking of the angels that sinned, presumably the origin of the demons that roam the world. God did not spare these angels but cast them down to hell and delivered into chains of darkness, reserved to judgment. But they aren't the only ones facing that judgment. Peter goes on to say, *"The Lord knoweth how to deliver the godly out of temptations, and to reserve the unjust unto the day of judgment to be punished" (2 Peter 2:9).*

There are two very different things that result from sin. One is the natural consequence of the sin. The other is punishment. But punishment requires due process, hence a day of judgment for a class of people. Peter describes them. *"Chiefly them that walk after the flesh in the lust of uncleanness, and despise government. Presumptuous are they, self willed, they are not afraid to speak evil of dignities" (v. 10).*

The unjust, in this passage, are a singular class of people, but they aren't far off from us. Peter says that they actually "feast with you," implying that they are associated with the church.

> *Having eyes full of adultery, and that cannot cease from sin; beguiling unstable souls: an heart they have exercised with covetous practices; cursed children: Which have forsaken the right way, and are gone astray. . .These are wells without water, clouds that are carried with a tempest; to whom the mist of darkness is reserved for ever. For when they speak great swelling words of vanity, they allure through the lusts of the flesh, through much wantonness, those that were clean escaped from them who live in error (2 Peter 2:14-18).*

It is a chilling image that Peter paints for us, but there should be a time when we think soberly about this. Rosh Hashana, the Feast of Trumpets, is a perfect time. And the church needs to hear it, because there are people *in the church* who fall squarely in this category, and a good part of the reason for their judgment is because they corrupt the church.

It isn't surprising that we find the same theme in the Psalms.

> *I will praise thee, O LORD, with my whole heart; I will show forth all thy marvellous works. I will be glad and rejoice in thee: I will sing praise to thy name, O thou most High. When mine enemies are turned back, they shall fall and perish at thy presence. For thou hast maintained my right and my cause; thou satest in the throne judging right . . . But the LORD shall endure for ever: he hath prepared his throne for judgment. And he shall judge the world in righteousness, he shall minister judgment to the people in uprightness (Psalm 9:1-8).*

The Psalm goes on to describe a time when God makes

inquisition for blood, and declares that Yahweh is "known by the judgment which he executes."

Later a Psalm also speaks of a judgment day; *"He shall call to the heavens from above, and to the earth, that he may judge his people. "*Even the heavens declare that *"God is judge himself" (Psalm 50:4).* The Psalms also connect the idea of trumpets and the judgment day.

> *With trumpets and sound of cornet make a joyful noise before the LORD, the King. Let the sea roar, and the fulness thereof; the world, and they that dwell therein. Let the floods clap their hands: let the hills be joyful together before the LORD; for he cometh to judge the earth: with righteousness shall he judge the world, and the people with equity" (Psalm 98:6-9).*

*"God shall, "*said Solomon in Ecclesiastes, *"bring every work into judgment and every secret thing, whether it be good or whether it be evil" (Ecclesiastes 12:14).* What Solomon doesn't say is the identity of the one doing the judging. It is perhaps surprising when we learn that it is not the Father who does the judging, but the Son. The Father, Jesus said, judges no man but has committed all judgment to the Son (John 5:22). *"My judgment is just, "* he went on to say, *"because I seek not mine own will, but the will of the Father which hath sent me."*

When Paul gave his great sermon on Mars Hill in Athens, he concluded that there is indeed a Judgment Day.

> *Forasmuch then as we are the offspring of God, we ought not to think that the Godhead is like unto gold, or silver, or stone, graven by art and man's device. And the times of this ignorance God winked at; but now commandeth all men every where to repent: Because he hath appointed a day, in the which he will judge the world in righteousness by that man whom he hath ordained; whereof he hath given assurance unto all men, in that he hath raised him from the dead (Acts 17:29-31).*

Not only has God appointed a day, he has appointed a judge, and that judge is none other than Jesus Christ. And since he is the Judge, we have no business judging one another:

> *But why dost thou judge thy brother? or why dost thou set at nought thy brother? for we shall all stand before the judgment seat of Christ. For it is written, As I live, saith the Lord, every knee shall bow to me, and every tongue shall confess to God. So then every one of us shall give account of himself to God (Romans 14:10-12).*

It is only in understanding the idea of *final judgment* that the Doctrine of Grace comes into play. For our Judge is the one who died for us. And in that great day, we will depend totally on his mercy. For there are no acts of righteousness we can do to make amends to him.

---

i. Judaism 101, http://www.jewfaq.org/holiday3.htm.

ii. See 2 Peter 2:4-22.

Printed in the United States
72041LV00005B/55-60